Ev

Every

Sweet Will Be
the Flower

Poems on Gardens

Selected and edited by DOUGLAS BROOKS-DAVIES

EVERYMAN

J. M. Dent · London

This edition first published by Everyman Paperbacks in 1999
Selection, introduction and other critical apparatus
© J. M. Dent 1999

J. M. Dent
Orion Publishing Group
Orion House
5 Upper St Martin's Lane
London WC2H 9EA

Typeset by Deltatype Ltd, Birkenhead, Merseyside
Printed in Great Britain by
The Guernsey Press Co. Ltd, Guernsey, C. I.

British Library Cataloguing-in-Publication
Data is available on request

ISBN 0 460 87996 0

Contents

Note on the Editor

DOUGLAS BROOKS-DAVIES was born in Wimbledon in 1942 and educated at Merchant Taylors' School, Crosby, and Brasenose College, Oxford. He was Senior Lecturer in English Literature at the University of Manchester until 1993 and is now an Honorary Research Fellow there. His hobbies include gardening and playing the oboe.

The founder editor of Manchester University Press's Literature in Context series, he has published widely on Renaissance, eighteenth- and nineteenth-century English literature. His books include *Number and Pattern in the Eighteenth-Century Novel* (Routledge, 1973); *Pope's 'Dunciad' and the Queen of Night* (Manchester U.P., 1985); *Oedipal Hamlet* (Macmillan, 1989). Among his editions are: *Silver Poets of the Sixteenth Century* (1992); *Spenser's 'Fairy Queen'* (1996) (both Dent); *Spenser: Selected Shorter Poems* (Longman, 1995); L.P. Hartley's *The Go-Between* (Penguin, 1997); and Henry Fielding's *Tom Jones* and Charlotte Brontë's *Jane Eyre* (both Dent, 1998). He has also edited *Alexander Pope* (1996), *Robert Herrick* (1996), *Four Metaphysical Poets* (1997) and *Jane Austen* (1998) for Everyman's Poetry.

Introduction

This anthology covers six centuries of poems about gardens, from the paradise garden of Chaucer's *Romance of the Rose* (his translation of the thirteenth-century French romance, *le Roman de la Rose*) to the subjective, and more threatening, inner gardens of Elizabeth Jennings and Anne Stevenson. It therefore offers brief, lyrical glimpses of garden history; even more, it demonstrates the very different functions that gardens have played, and continue to play, in our conscious and unconscious minds.

First, the history. Chaucer's translation of the *Roman de la Rose* gives us a glimpse of the voguish walled paradise garden (from the Greek *paradeisos* = an enclosed park), combining elements of the enclosed Persian desert garden and pleasure garden or *locus amoenus*; Pope celebrates André Le Nôtre's contribution to Versailles and the work of Bridgeman and Kent at Stowe, championing the designer who has an intuitive feel for the landscape in the figure of the guardian deity of the place (*Genius loci*) rather than the one who merely turns up with his plans and teams of labourers, digging up, replanting and building with regard for drawing board rather than nature; George Meredith sides with the many who, in Victorian England, rejected the taste for the exotic and the most rarefied hybrid when he eschews the 'prim' garden flowers 'trained to stand in rows, and asking if they please' for his beloved 'wild ones. / O my wild ones! they tell me more than these' (*Love in the Valley*). Then, too, we have Cowper celebrating the advantages of a heated greenhouse and poking fun at 'Capability' Brown (*The Task*, Book III) or, in the modern period, brisk advice about planting for seasonal colour: 'But for this summer's quick delight / Sow marigold, and sow the bright / Frail poppy' (Vita Sackville-West, *The Land*).

Beyond the planning, satisfaction, excitement and backache, however, gardening – like angling – provokes a certain elegiac and practical, homespun philosophising. Gardens live and metamorphose, but the all-too mortal gardener has to work within time for posterity, as Sackville-West's narrator reminds us: 'Sow . . . Not for this summer, but for next, / Since foresight is the gardener's text', and although he may not be alive to see them, 'Others will stand and musing say / "These were the flowers he sowed that May" '. A similar, yet more urgently personal, note is struck by Mary Ursula Bethell: ' "Established" is a good word, much used in garden books . . . Oh, become established quickly, quickly, garden! / For I am fugitive, I am very fugitive' ('Time').

Those who know the *Romance of the Rose* will be aware, nevertheless, that Chaucer's garden is also a dream vision, and that it culminates in the image of the unattainable beloved as a rose. So Chaucer's paradise garden is no less subjective than those of much more modern poets. This is scarcely surprising, since the inner garden has existed as long as poetry itself, from the garden of Eden when understood as representing a spiritual and moral state as well as objective place (what John Milton calls 'the paradise within' (*Paradise Lost* (1667; 1674), XII. 587)); its Greek parallel in the garden of Alcinous in Homer's *Odyssey* (which signifies a visionary and longed-for moment of stasis and beauty wrested from the turmoils of Ulysses' storm-tossed and threatening voyage home); to Margaret Cavendish's extraordinary *paysage moralisé* of 'A Landscape' (the elliptical syntax of which echoes the mistiness of a perception that really is unsure whether the topography is that of objective landscape or a solipsistic inner eye) and Walter de la Mare's 'Sunken Garden', with its dreamy and ghostly memories of long-gone children summed up in the haunting statue of its solitary guardian boy.

But, as I have already implied by mentioning Eden, these subjective gardens are themselves often dependent on myth and legend.

For Chaucer's rose-maiden is at once the seductive daughter of Venus (to whom the rose was anciently dedicated) and the unattainable Virgin Mary, whom medieval iconography saw as a rose at the centre of her own symbolic enclosed garden, the *hortus conclusus* (see Eithne Wilkins, *The Rose-Garden Game* (London: Gollancz, 1969)). Then again, the Elizabethan knot-garden was a stylised maze, emblem of life's moral perplexity, of error (from Latin *errare* = to deviate from the straight path) questing for truth: there hadn't, therefore, been a maze in the garden of Eden until, as Milton again puts it, the Satanic serpent approached Eve 'on his rear, / Circular base of rising folds, that towered / Fold above fold a surging maze, his head / Crested aloft' (*Paradise Lost*, IX. 497–500). Moreover, grafting and hybridisation were part of the continuing dialogue between man and nature that had been set up since the Fall of man and Adam and Eve's expulsion from the garden (Genesis 3) when, it was thought, nature, too, had fallen into imperfection. 'Create perfection and regain untainted prelapsarian nature' was the cry of the breeders; 'leave well alone because in interfering with the natural order you are creating bastard images of your own corruption' went the cry of the conservatives (see Marvell's 'The Mower against Gardens'). So, as we gather fruit from our thornless blackberries, we are benefiting from a breeding programme that has undone God's punishment in Genesis 3:17–18: 'cursed is the ground for thy sake . . . Thorns also and thistles shall it bring forth to thee' (though I suspect few of us are aware of that). The garden of Eden, then, is rarely absent from the poems in this anthology: implicit in Chaucer, it is explicit in Spenser's 'Garden of Adonis', and many other poems right through to Sir Henry Newbolt's sweetly elegiac 'Song', with its delicate ambiguity over Eve / evening in 'The stir of Morning's eager breath – / Beautiful Eve's impassioned death . . .'.

Underlying the biblical Eden is the classical Golden Age, that mythical moment in the earth's history when all was just and harmonious and man was in accord with nature to the extent that she fed him voluntarily. It informs the garden of Homer's Alcinous, while Drayton draws on this in the extract from his *Endymion and Phoebe*, and it is an element in all the classicising poets represented here through to Pope, Mason and Arnold. Yet when Pope translated it, it had a specific historical meaning: King Alcinous's ordered and fertile plot represented, like the landscape in Pope's almost contemporary *Windsor Forest*, England prosperous under the Stuart Queen Anne. Which reminds us that at least from the Middle Ages the realm-as-garden metaphor had been a potent one, particularly so at times of war or social disorder. It is out of this metaphor that Elizabeth I as supreme Tudor rose emerges (Sir John Davies's *Hymn*), and to which the Eden gardens of Marvell and Milton belong, images as they are of an ordered republic ordained by God for his chosen people.

And if the Golden Age and paradise, those gardens from the infancy of the world and of occidental literature, engender visions of political order, they can also encourage a very acute nostalgia for our lost childhood self. Robert Louis Stevenson feels obliged to write a whole *Child's Garden of Verses*; Anne Brontë cries out, in 'Home', for the wild landscape of her native Yorkshire, where she can be free from the imprisonment of employment in a mansion with its oppressively formal gardens and identify with her young self; some years earlier, Susan Blamire, in characteristically late eighteenth-century fashion, laments the lost garden of childhood, violated as it has been by the 'improvers' ('When Home We Return'), anticipating in tone and content Thomas Moore's ''Tis the Last Rose of Summer', that elegy for lost love, friends and family with its need to die with those one grieves for.

This particular elegiac strand finds its supreme expression in Tennyson's *In Memoriam* and, more formally, in Arnold's *Thyrsis*. Yet, even as both poets touch a peak of private grief, they hark back to the ancient Greek elegies of Bion, Theocritus and Moschus, with their bereft flower-strewn landscapes and Adonis gardens.

Tennyson's *In Memoriam*, like Chaucer's *Romance of the Rose* translation is, of course, also in the long tradition of garden love poems. The idealised rose-maiden, beloved as well as queen, in the medieval poem 'This day day daws' (with her overtones of the Virgin Mary as the enclosed garden of Song of Solomon 4:12) leads us on through Thomas Howell's 'The Rose', Spenser's 'Coming to Kiss her Lips', and Campion's 'There is a Garden in Her Face' to practically every love poem written since. However, the 'roses and white lilies' of Campion's first stanza come from Song of Solomon 2:1–2 ('I am the rose of Sharon and the lily of the valleys. As the lily among thorns, so is my love among the daughters'): a complicating factor to the apparent simplicities of the poem, and one which reminds us, in turn, that the symbolic and mythological language of flowers lies at the root of most garden poems. Primroses signify youth, innocence, virginity and also youth's lewdness (as in Vaughan's 'Regeneration', st. 1); roses, as we have seen, belong to Venus (but also, in medieval tradition, the Virgin Mary) and signify love but also transience; violets suggest maidenly modesty and humility; columbine (its name derives from its dovelike petals: Latin *columba* = dove) is equally ambivalent, symbolising on the one hand love and Venus, one of whose attributes is the dove, and on the other the Holy Spirit (e.g., Matthew 3:16). All of which is to say that gardens – and garden poems and paintings – have meanings: they are mystic, resonating spaces.

Finally, I thank everyone who has helped me with advice for this selection, particularly Grevel Lindop. I hope that it contains what every garden – however small – should: something to delight everyone.

DOUGLAS BROOKS-DAVIES

Note on the Texts

Where necessary, I have given sources for texts used in the Notes. Spelling and punctuation have been modernised, except in the case of works written over the past century or so.

Note on the Text

Sweet Will Be the Flower

GEOFFREY CHAUCER

The Garden of Mirth

The garden was, by measuring,
Right even and square in compassing:
It as long was as it was large.
Of fruit had every tree his charge,
But it were any hideous tree,   5
Of which there were two or three.
There were – and that wot I full well –
Of pomegranates a full great deal:
That is a fruit full well to like,
Namely to folk when they been sick.   10
And trees there were, great foison,
That bearen nuts in their season,
Such as men nutmegs call,
That sweet of savour been withal.
And alemanders great plenty,   15
Figs, and many a date tree
There waxen, if men had need,
Through the garden in length and breadth.
There was eke waxing many a spice,
As clove-gillyflower, and liquorice,   20
Ginger, and Grain de Parays,
Canel, and cetewale of price,
And many a spice delectable
To eaten when men rise from table.
And many homely trees there were   25
That peaches, quinces, and apples bare,
Medlars, plums, pears, chestnuts,
Cherries, of which many one fain is;
Nuts, aleys, and bullaces,
That for to seen it was solace.   30
With many high laurel and pine
Was ranged clean all that garden,
With cypress and with olivers,

Of which that nigh no plenty here is.
There were elms great and strong,   35
Maples, ash, oak, asp, planes long,
Fine yew, poplar, and lindens fair,
And other trees full many a pair . . .
　　In places saw I wells there,
In which there no frogs were,   40
And fair in shade was every well,
But I ne can the number tell . . .
Through moisture of the well wet
Sprang up the sweet green grass
As fair, as thick, as mister was;   45
But much amended it the place
That the earth was of such a grace
That it of flowers hath plenty
That both in summer and winter be.
　　There sprang the violet all new,   50
And fresh periwink, rich of hue,
And flowers yellow, white and red:
Such plenty grew there never in mead.
Full gay was all the ground, and quaint,
And powdered (as men had it paint)   55
With many a fresh and sundry flower
That casten up full good savour . . .

ANON

Mum and the Soothsayer

Then leaped I forth lightly and looked about,
And I beheld a fair house with halls and chambers,
A franklin's freehold, all fresh new.
I bent me about and bode at the door
Of the gladdest garden that gome ever had.   5
I have no time, truly, to tell all the names
Of imps and herbs and other fele things

That growed on that garden, the ground was so noble.
I passed in privily and pulled off the fruits,
And roamed the alleys round all about;   10
But so seemly a sage as I saw there
I saw not, soothly, sith I was bore:
An old, ancient man of a hundred winter . . .
'I am gardener of this garth,' quoth he, 'the ground is mine
own
For to dig and to delve and to do such deeds   15
As longeth to this leighton; the law woll I do,
And root up the weeds that ruin my plants;
And worms that worken not but wasten my herbs,
I dash them to death, and delve out their dens.
But the drones doen worst – die mote they all: 20
They haunten the hive for money that is in,
And lurken, and licken the liquor that is sweet,
And travailen no twint, but taken of the best
Of that the bees bringen from blossoms and flowers.
For of all the beasts that breeden upon earth,   25
For quality ne quantity, no question, I trow,
The bee in his business best is allowed,
And proveth in his propriety passing all other,
And prettiest in his working to profit of the people.'

WILLIAM DUNBAR

'Sweet Rose of Virtue'

Sweet rose of virtue and of gentleness,
Delightsome lily of every lustiness,
    Richest in bounty and in beauty clear,
    And every virtue that is held most dear –
Except only that ye are merciless.   5

Into your garth this day I did pursue;
There saw I flowers that fresh were of hue,

Both white and red most lusty were to seen,
And wholesome herbs upon stalkès green –
Yet leaf nor flower could find I none of rue.   10

I doubt that March with his cold blasts keen
Has slain this gentle herb that I of mene,
    Whose piteous death does to my heart such pain
    That I would make to plant his root again,
So comfortand his leaves unto me been.   15

JOHN SKELTON

To Mistress Isabel Pennell

By Saint Mary, my lady,
Your mammy and your daddy
Brought forth a goodly baby.

My maiden Isabel,
Reflairing rosabel,   5
The fragrant camomel,

The ruddy rosary,
The sovereign rosemary,
The pretty strawberry,

The columbine, the nept,   10
The gillyflower well set,
The proper violet.

Ennewed your colour
Is like the daisy flower
After the April shower,   15

Star of the morrow grey,
The blossom on the spray,
The freshest flower of May,

Maidenly demure,
Of womanhood the lure;   20
Wherefore I you assure,

It were an heavenly health,
It were an endless wealth,
A life for God himself,

To hear this nightingale   25
Among the birdès small
Warbling in the vale,

'Dug, dug,
Jug, jug!
Good year and good luck!'   30
With 'Chuck, chuck, chuck, chuck!'

ANON

'This day day daws'

'This day day daws,
This gentle day day daws,
This gentle day daws,
And I must home gone.'

In a glorious garden green   5
Saw I sitting a comely queen
Among the flowers that fresh been.
She gathered a flower and sat between:
    The lily-white rose methought I saw,
    The lily-white rose methought I saw,   10
        And ever she sang:

'This day day daws . . .'

In that garden be flowers of hue:
The gillyflower gent, that she well knew;
The flower-de-luce she did on rue,   15
And said: 'The white rose is most true
    This garden to rule by righteous law.'
    The lily-white rose methought I saw,
        And ever she sang:

    'This day day daws . . .'

THOMAS HOWELL

The Rose

Whenas the mildest month
    Of jolly June doth spring,
And gardens green with happy hue
    Their famous fruits do bring;
When eke the lustiest time   5
    Reviveth youthly blood,
Then springs the finest featured flower
    In border fair that stood:
Which moveth me to say,
    In time of pleasant year,   10
Of all the pleasant flowers in June
    The red rose hath no peer.

GEORGE GASCOIGNE

Inscription in a Garden

If any flower that here is grown,
　Or any herb, may ease your pain,
Take, and account it as your own,
　　But recompense the like again:
　　　For some and some is honest play,   5
　　　And so my wife taught me to say.

If here to walk you take delight,
　Why, come, and welcome, when you will;
If I bid you sup here this night,
　　Bid me another time, and still   10
　　　Think some and some is honest play,
　　　For so my wife taught me to say.

Thus, if you sup or dine with me,
　If you walk here or sit at ease,
If you desire the thing you see,   15
　　And have the time your mind to please,
　　　Think some and some is honest play,
　　　And so my wife taught me to say.

EDMUND SPENSER

The Garden of Adonis

She brought her to her joyous paradise
　Where most she wones when she on earth does dwell –
So fair a place as Nature can devise:
　Whether in Paphos, or Cytheron hill,
　Or it in Gnidus be, I wote not well.   5
　But well I wote by trial that this same

All other pleasant places doth excel,
And called is by her lost lover's name
The Garden of Adonis, far renowned by fame.

In that same garden all the goodly flowers   10
Wherewith Dame Nature doth her beautify,
And decks the garlands of her paramours,
Are fetched. There is the first seminary
Of all things that are born to live and die
According to their kinds. Long work it were   15
Here to account the endless progeny
Of all the weeds that bud and blossom there:
But so much as doth need must needs be counted here.

It sited was in fruitful soil of old,
And girt in with two walls on either side,   20
The one of iron, the other of bright gold,
That none might through break nor overstride.
And double gates it had which opened wide
By which both in and out men moten pass –
The one fair and fresh, the other old and dried.   25
Old Genius the porter of them was –
Old Genius, the which a double nature has.

He letteth in, he letteth out to wend
All that to come into the world desire:
A thousand thousand naked babes attend   30
About him day and night, which do require
That he with fleshly weeds would them attire.
Such as him list, such as eternal Fate
Ordained hath, he clothes with sinful mire
And sendeth forth to live in mortal state   35
Till they again return back by the hinder gate.

After that they again returned been,
They in that garden planted be again
And grow afresh, as they had never seen
Fleshly corruption nor mortal pain.   40
Some thousand years so doen they there remain,
And then of him are clad with other hue,

Or sent into the changeful world again
  Till thither they return where first they grew:
So like a wheel around they run from old to new.   45

Ne needs there gardener to set or sow,
  To plant or prune for, of their own accord,
  All things as they created were do grow,
  And yet remember well the mighty word
  Which first was spoken by the Almighty Lord   50
  That bade them to increase and multiply.
  Ne do they need with water of the ford
  Or of the clouds to moisten their roots dry,
For in themselves eternal moisture they imply.

Infinite shapes of creatures there are bred,   55
  And uncouth forms which none yet ever knew,
  And every sort is in a sundry bed
  Set by itself and ranked in comely row:
  Some fit for reasonable souls to endue,
  Some made for breasts, some made for birds to wear,   60
  And all the fruitful spawn of fishes' hue
  In endless ranks along enranged were
That seemed the ocean could not contain them there.

Daily they grow, and daily forth are sent
  Into the world it to replenish more: 65
  Yet is the stock not lessened, nor spent,
  But still remains in everlasting store
  As it at first created was of yore.
  For in the wide womb of the world there lies,
  In hateful darkness and in deep horror,   70
  An huge eternal Chaos which supplies
The substances of Nature's faithful progenies.

All things from thence do their first being fetch
  And borrow matter, whereof they are made,
  Which, whenas form and feature it does catch,   75
  Becomes a body and doth then invade
  The state of life out of the grisly shade.
  That substance is etern', and bideth so;

Ne when the life decays and form does fade
　　Doth it consume and into nothing go, 　　　　80
But changed is, and often altered to and fro.

The substance is not changed nor altered,
　　But the only form and outward fashion;
　　For every substance is conditioned
　　To change her hue and sundry forms to don, 　　85
　　Meet for her temper and complexion.
　　For forms are variable, and decay
　　By course of kind and by occasion,
　　And that fair flower of beauty fades away
As doth the lily fresh before the sunny ray. 　　90

Great enemy to it and to all the rest
　　That in the Garden of Adonis springs
　　Is wicked Time, who, with his scythe addressed,
　　Does mow the flowering herbs and goodly things
　　And all their glory to the ground down flings, 　　95
　　Where they do wither and are foully marred.
　　He flies about and, with his flaggy wings,
　　Beats down both leaves and buds without regard,
Ne ever pity may relent his malice hard.

Ye pity often did the gods relent 　　　　　　100
　　To see so fair things marred and spoiled quite,
　　And their great mother, Venus, did lament
　　The loss of her dear brood, her dear delight:
　　Her heart was pierced with pity at the sight
　　When, walking through the garden, them she spied, 　105
　　Yet n'ote she find redress for such despite.
　　For all that lives in subject to that law:
All things decay in time, and to their end do draw.

But were it not that Time their troubler is,
　　All that in this delightful garden grows 　　　110
　　Should happy be and have immortal bliss:
　　For here all plenty and all pleasure flows,
　　And sweet love gentle fits amongst them throws
　　Without fell rancour or fond jealousy.

Frankly each paramour his leman knows,   115
    Each bird his mate, ne any does envy
Their goodly merriment and gay felicity.

There is continual spring, and harvest there
    Continual, both meeting at one time;
    For both the boughs do laughing blossoms bare   120
    And with fresh colours deck the wanton prime;
    And eke at once the heavy trees they climb
    Which seem to labour under their fruits' load –
    The whiles the joyous birds make their pastime
    Amongst the shady leaves (their sweet abode)   125
And their true loves without suspicion tell abroad . . .

Sonnet: 'Coming to Kiss her Lips . . .'

Coming to kiss her lips, such grace I found,
    Me seemed I smelled a garden of sweet flowers
    That dainty odours from them threw around
    For damsels fit to deck their lovers' bowers:
Her lips did smell like unto gillyflowers;   5
    Her ruddy cheeks like unto roses red;
    Her snowy brows like budded bellamours;
    Her lovely cheeks like pinks but newly spread;
Her goodly bosom like a strawberry bed;
    Her neck like to a bunch of columbines;   10
Her breast like lilies ere their leaves be shed;
    Her nipples like young-blossomed jessamines:
Such fragrant flowers do give most odorous smell,
    But her sweet odour did them all excel.

GEORGE CHAPMAN

from Ovid's Banquet of Sense

And thus to bathing came our poet's goddess,
   Her handmaids bearing all things pleasure yields
To such a service – odours most delighted,
And purest linen which her looks had whited.

Then cast she off her robe and stood upright: 5
As lightning breaks out of a labouring cloud;
Or as the morning heaven casts off the night;
Or as that heaven cast off itself and showed
   Heaven's upper light, to which the brightest day
Is but a black and melancholy shroud;   10
   Or as when Venus strived for sovereign sway
Of charmful beauty in young Troy's desire:
So stood Corinna vanishing her tire.

A soft enflowered bank embraced the fount,
Of Chloris' ensigns an abstracted field,   15
Where grew melanthy, great in bees' account;
Amareus, that precious balm doth yield;
   Enamelled pansies, used at nuptials still;
Dian's arrow; Cupid's crimson shield;
   Ope-morn; nightshade; and Venus' navel;   20
Solemn violets, hanging head as shamed;
And verdant calamint, for odour famed;

Sacred nepenthe, purgative of care;
And sovereign rumex, that doth rancour kill;
Sya; and hyacinth, that Furies wear;   25
White and red jessamines; merry; melliphill.
   Fair crown imperial, emperor of flowers;
Immortal amaranth; white asphodel;
   And cup-like twillpants, strewed in Bacchus' bowers –
These cling about this Nature's naked gem,   30
To taste her sweets, as bees do swarm on them . . .

MICHAEL DRAYTON

from **Endymion and Phoebe**

Upon this mount there stood a stately grove,
Whose reaching arms to clip the welkin strove,
Of tufted cedars and the branching pine,
Whose bushy tops themselves do so entwine
As seemed, when Nature first this work began,   5
She then conspired against the piercing sun;
Under whose covert (thus divinely made)
Phoebus' green laurel flourished in the shade,
Fair Venus' myrtle, Mars his warlike fir,
Minerva's olive, and the weeping myrrh,   10
The patient palm, which thrives in spite of hate,
The poplar, to Alcides consecrate;
Which Nature in such order had disposed,
And therewithal these goodly walks enclosed,
As served for hangings and rich tapestry   15
To beautify this stately gallery.
Embroidering these, in curious trails along,
The clustered grapes and golden citrons hung:
More glorious than the precious fruit were these
Kept by the dragon in Hesperides,   20
Or gorgeous arras in rich colours wrought
With silk from Afric or from Indy brought.
Out of this soil sweet bubbling fountains crept,
As though for joy the senseless stones had wept,
With straying channels dancing sundry ways,   25
With often turns, like to a curious maze;
Which, breaking forth, the tender grass bedewed,
Whose silver sand with orient pearl was strewed,
Shadowed with roses and sweet eglantine,
Dipping their sprays into this crystalline;   30
From which the birds the purple berries pruned,
And to their loves their small recorders tuned:
The nightingale, woods' herald of the spring,
The whistling ouzel, mavis carolling,
Tuning their trebles to the waters' fall,   35

Which made their music more angelical;
Whilst gentle Zephyr, murmuring among,
Kept time, and bore the burden to the song:
About whose brims, refreshed with dainty showers,
Grew amaranthus and sweet gillyflowers,   40
The marigold, Phoebus' beloved friend,
The moly, which from sorcery doth defend,
Violet, carnation, balm and cassia,
Idea's primrose, coronet of may . . .

WILLIAM SHAKESPEARE

Boy's Song

Roses, their sharp spines being gone,
Not royal in their smells alone,
   But in their hue;
Maiden pinks, of odour faint,
Daisies smell-less, yet most quaint,   5
   And sweet thyme true;

Primrose, firstborn child of Ver,
Merry springtime's harbinger,
   With harebells dim;
Oxlips in their cradles growing,   10
Marigolds on death-beds blowing,
   Larks'-heels trim:

All dear Nature's children sweet
Lie 'fore bride and bridegroom's feet,
   Blessing their sense;   15
Not an angel of the air,
Bird melodious or bird fair,
   Is absent hence.

The crow, the slanderous cuckoo, nor
The boding raven, nor chough hoar,
   Nor chattering pie,
May on our bride-house perch or sing,
Or with them any discord bring,
   But from it fly.

20

THOMAS CAMPION

'There is a Garden in Her Face'

There is a garden in her face
Where roses and white lilies grow;
   A heavenly paradise is that place,
Wherein all pleasant fruits do flow.
   There cherries grow which none may buy,
   Till 'cherry ripe' themselves do cry.

5

Those cherries fairly do enclose
Of orient pearls a double row,
   Which, when her lovely laughter shows,
They look like rosebuds filled with snow.
   Yet them nor peer nor prince can buy,
   Till 'cherry ripe' themselves do cry.

10

Her eyes like angels watch them still,
Her brows like bended bows do stand,
   Threatening with piercing frowns to kill
All that attempt with eye or hand
   Those sacred cherries to come nigh,
   Till 'cherry ripe' themselves do cry.

15

SIR JOHN DAVIES

from **Hymns of Astraea**

E ye of the garden, queen of flowers,
L ove's cup wherein he nectar pours,
I ngendered first of nectar;
S weet nurse-child of the spring's young Hours
A nd beauty's fair character;   5

B est jewel that the earth doth wear,
E ven when the brave young sun draws near,
T o her hot love pretending;
H imself likewise like form doth bear
A t rising and descending;   10

R ose, of the queen of love beloved:
E ngland's great kings, divinely moved,
G ave roses in their banner;
I t showed that Beauty's rose indeed
N ow in this age should them succeed,   15
A nd reign in more sweet manner.

AEMILIA LANYER

The Description of Cookham

Farewell, sweet Cookham, where I first obtained
Grace from that Grace where perfect grace remained,
And where the Muses gave their full consent
I should have power the virtuous to content;
Where princely palace willed me to indite   5
The sacred story of the soul's delight.
Farewell, sweet place, where Virtue then did rest,
And all delights did harbour in her breast:

Never shall my sad eyes again behold
Those pleasures which my thoughts did then unfold.   10
Yet you, great lady, mistress of that place,
From whose desire did spring this work of grace,
Vouchsafe to think upon those pleasures past
As fleeting worldly joys that could not last,
Or as dim shadows of celestial pleasures   15
Which are desired above all earthly treasures,
Oh how (me thought) against you hither came,
Each part did seem some new delight to frame!
The house received all ornaments to grace it,
And would endure no foulness to deface it;   20
The walks put on their summer liveries,
And all things else did hold like similes:
The trees with leaves, with fruits, with flowers, clad,
Embraced each other, seeming to be glad,
Turning themselves to beauteous canopies   25
To shade the bright sun from your brighter eyes;
The crystal streams with silver spangles graced
While by the glorious sun they were embraced;
The little birds in chirping notes did sing
To entertain both you and that sweet spring;   30
And Philomela with her sundry lays
Both you and that delightful place did praise.
Oh how me thought each plant, each flower, each tree,
Set forth their beauties then to welcome thee!
The very hills right humbly did descend   35
When you to tread upon them did intend.
And, as you set your feet, they still did rise,
Glad that they could receive so rich a prize.
The gentle winds did take delight to be
Among those woods that were so graced by thee,   40
And in sad murmur uttered pleasing sound
That pleasure in that place might more abound.
The swelling banks delivered all their pride
When such a phoenix once they had espied;
Each arbour, bank, each seat, each stately tree,   45
Thought themselves honoured in supporting thee.
The pretty birds would oft come to attend thee,
Yet fly away for fear they should offend thee;

The little creatures in the burrow by
Would come abroad to sport them in your eye,   50
Yet, fearful of the bow in your fair hand,
Would run away when you did make a stand.
Now let me come unto that stately tree
Wherein such goodly prospects you did see:
That oak that did in height his fellows pass   55
As much as lofty trees low-growing grass:
Much like a comely cedar, straight and tall,
Whose beauteous stature far exceeded all.
How often did you visit this fair tree
Which, seeming joyful in receiving thee,   60
Would like a palm tree spread his arms abroad,
Desirous that you there should make abode;
Whose fair green leaves, much like a comely veil,
Defended Phoebus when he would assail;
Whose pleasing boughs did yield a cool, fresh air,   65
Joying his happiness when you were there,
Where, being seated, you might plainly see
Hills, vales, and woods (as if on bended knee
They had appeared, your honour to salute,
Or to prefer some strange, unlooked for, suit),   70
All interlaced with brooks and crystal springs,
A prospect fit to please the eyes of kings.
And thirteen shires appeared in all your sight:
Europe could not afford much more delight.
What was there then but gave you all content,   75
While you the time in meditation spent,
Of their Creator's power, which there you saw,
In all his creatures held a perfect law.
And in their beauties did you plain descry
His beauty, wisdom, grace, love, majesty . . .   80
And you, sweet Cookham, whom these ladies leave,
I now must tell the grief you did conceive
At their departure; when they went away,
How everything retained a sad dismay.
Nay, long before, when once an inkling came,   85
Me thought each thing did unto sorrow frame.
The trees, that were so glorious in our view,
Forsook both flowers and fruit when once they knew

Of your depart; their very leaves did wither,
Changing their colours as they grew together.   90
But when they saw this had no power to stay you,
They often wept (though, speechless, could not pray you),
Letting their tears in your fair bosom fall,
As if they said, 'Why will ye leave us all?'
This being vain, they cast their leaves away,   95
Hoping that pity would have made you stay:
Their frozen tops, like Age's hoary hairs,
Shows their disaster languishing in fears;
A swarthy, rivelled rind all over spread
Their dying bodies half-alive, half-dead . . .   100
The sun grew weak, his beams no comfort gave,
While all green things did make the earth their grave.
Each brier, each bramble, when you went away
Caught fast your clothes, thinking to make you stay;
Delightful Echo, wonted to reply   105
To our last words, did now for sorrow die;
The house cast off each garment that might grace it,
Putting on dust and cobwebs to deface it:
All desolation then there did appear
When you were going, whom they held so dear.   110
This last farewell to Cookham here I give;
When I am dead thy name in this may live
Wherein I have performed her noble hest
Whose virtues lodge in my unworthy breast:
And ever shall, so long as life remains,   115
Tying my heart to her by those rich chains.

BEN JONSON

To Penshurst

Thou art not, Penshurst, built to envious show
    Of touch or marble; nor canst boast a row
Of polished pillars, or a roof of gold;
    Thou hast no lantern whereof tales are told,

Or stair, or courts; but stand'st an ancient pile,   5
    And these grudged at, art reverenced the while.
Thou joyest in better marks, of soil, of air,
    Of wood, of water: therein thou art fair.
Thou hast thy walks for health, as well as sport;
    Thy mount, to which the dryads do resort,   10
Where Pan and Bacchus their high feasts have made
    Beneath the broad beech and the chestnut shade;
That taller tree which of a nut was set
    At his great birth, where all the Muses met.
There, in the writhed bark, are cut the names   15
    Of many a sylvan taken with his flames.
And thence the ruddy satyrs oft provoke
    The lighter fauns to reach thy lady's oak.
Thy copse, too, named of Gamage, thou hast there,
    That never fails to serve the seasoned deer,   20
Where thou wouldst feast or exercise thy friends.
    The lower land, that to the river bends,
Thy sheep, thy bullocks, kine, and calves do feed;
    The middle ground thy mares and horses breed.
Each bank doth yield thee conies, and the tops   25
    Fertile of wood – Ashore, and Sidney's copse –
To crown thy open table doth provide
    The purpled pheasant with the speckled side.
The painted partridge lies in every field
    And, for thy mess, is willing to be killed.   30
And if the high-swollen Medway fail thy dish,
    Thou hast thy ponds that pay thee tribute fish:
Fat, aged carps, that run into thy net;
    And pikes, now weary their own kind to eat,
As loth the second cast or draught to stay,   35
    Officiously at first themselves betray;
Bright eels, that emulate them and leap on land
    Before the fisher, or into his hand.
Then hath thy orchard fruit, thy garden flowers,
    Fresh as the air, and new as are the Hours: 40
The early cherry, with the later plum,
    Fig, grape, and quince, each in his time doth come;
The blushing apricot and woolly peach
    Hang on thy walls, that every child may reach.

And though thy walls be of the country stone,   45
    They're reared with no man's ruin, no man's groan:
There's none that dwell about them wish them down,
    But all come in, the farmer and the clown –
And no one empty-handed – to salute
    Thy lord and lady, though they have no suit.   50
Some bring a capon, some a rural cake,
    Some nuts, some apples; some that think they make
The better cheeses, bring them, or else send
    By their ripe daughters whom they would commend
This way to husbands, and whose baskets bear   55
    An emblem of themselves in plum or pear.
But what can this (more than express their love)
    Add to thy free provisions, far above
The need of such? whose liberal board doth flow
    With all that hospitality doth know;   60
Where comes no guest but is allowed to eat
    Without his fear and of thy lord's own meat;
Where the same beer, and bread, and self-same wine
    That is his lordship's, shall be also mine,
And I not fain to sit (as some, this day,   65
    At great men's tables), and yet dine away.
Here no man tells my cups nor, standing by,
    A waiter doth my gluttony envy,
But gives me what I call, and lets me eat:
    He knows below he shall find plenty of meat.   70
Thy tables hoard not up for the next day,
    Nor, when I take my lodging, need I pray
For fire or lights or livery: all is there
    As if thou, then, wert mine, and I reigned here:
There's nothing I can wish for which I stay.   75
    That found King James when, hunting late this way
With his brave son, the prince, they saw thy fires
    Shine bright on every hearth, as the desires
Of thy penates had been set on flame
    To entertain them, or the country came,   80
Will all their zeal, to warm their welcome here:
    What – 'great' I will not say, but – sudden cheer
Didst thou then make them! And what praise was heaped
    On thy good lady, then, who therein reaped

The just reward on her high housewifery: 85
  To have her linen, plate, and all things, nigh
When she was far; and not a room but dressed
  As if it had expected such a guest!
These, Penshurst, are thy praise, and yet not all.
  Thy lady's noble, fruitful, chaste withal: 90
His children thy great lord may call his own
  (A fortune in this age but rarely known).
They are, and have been, taught religion: thence
  Their gentler spirits have sucked innocence;
Each morn and even they are taught to pray   95
  With the whole household, and may, every day,
Read in their virtuous parents' noble parts
  The mysteries of manners, arms and arts.
Now, Penshurst, they that will proportion thee
  With other edifices, when they see   100
Those proud, ambitious heaps, and nothing else,
  May say, their lords have built, but thy lord dwells.

WILLIAM BROWNE OF TAVISTOCK

Vision V

A rose, as fair as ever saw the north,
Grew in a little garden all alone;
A sweeter flower did Nature ne'er put forth,
Nor fairer garden yet was never known.
The maidens danced about it morn and noon,   5
And learned bards of it their ditties made;
The nimble fairies by the pale-faced moon
Watered the root and kissed her pretty shade.
But well-a-day, the gardener careless grew:
The maids and fairies both were kept away,   10
And in a drought the caterpillars threw
Themselves upon the bud and every spray.
    God shield the stock! If heaven send no supplies,
    The fairest blossom of the garden dies.

ROBERT HERRICK

A Meditation for His Mistress

You are a tulip seen today,
But (dearest) of so short a stay
That where you grew, scarce man can say.

You are a lovely July-flower,
Yet one rude wind, or ruffling shower,   5
Will force you hence, and in an hour.

You are a sparkling rose in the bud,
Yet lost ere that chaste flesh and blood
Can show where you grew or stood.

You are a full-spread fair-set vine,   10
And can with tendrils love entwine,
Yet dried, ere you distil your wine.

You are like balm enclosed well
In amber, or some crystal shell,
Yet lost ere you transfuse your smell.   15

You are a dainty violet,
Yet withered ere you can be set
Within the virgin's coronet.

You are the queen all flowers among,
But die you must, fair maid, ere long,   20
As he, the maker of this song.

To the most fair and lovely mistress, Anne Soame, now Lady Abdie

So smell those odours that do rise
From out the wealthy spiceries;
So smells the flower of blooming clove,
Or roses smothered in the stove;
So smells the air of spiced wine,   5
Or essences of jessamine;
So smells the breath about the hives
When well the work of honey thrives,
And all the busy factors come
Laden with wax and honey home.   10
So smell those neat and woven bowers
All over-arched with orange flowers;
And almond-blossoms, that do mix
To make rich these aromatics;
So smell those bracelets and those bands   15
Of amber chafed between the hands
When, thus enkindled, they transpire
A noble perfume from the fire.
The wine of cherries – and, to these,
The cooling breath of raspberries;   20
The smell of morning milk and cream,
Butter of cowslips mixed with them;
Of roasted warden or baked pear:
These are not to be reckoned here
Whenas the meanest part of her   25
Smells like the maiden pomander.
Thus sweet she smells, or what can be
More liked by her, or loved by me.

Christ's Sadness

Christ was not sad in the garden for His own
Passion, but for his sheeps' dispersion.

GEORGE HERBERT

Paradise

I bless thee, Lord, because I GROW
Among thy trees, which in a ROW
To thee both fruit and order OW.

What open force, or hidden CHARM,
Can blast my fruit, or bring me HARM,   5
While the enclosure is thine   ARM?

Enclose me still for fear I   START.
Be to me rather sharp and   TART
Than let me want thy hand and ART.

When thou dost greater judgements SPARE,   10
And with thy knife but prune and PARE,
Even fruitful trees more fruitful   ARE.

Such sharpness shows the sweetest FREND;
Such cuttings rather heal than   REND;
And such beginnings touch their   END.   15

Peace

Sweet Peace, where dost thou dwell? I humbly crave,
        Let me once know.
     I sought thee in a secret cave,
      And asked if Peace were there:
A hollow wind did seem to answer, 'No;   5
        Go seek elsewhere'.

I did; and, going, did a rainbow note.
        'Surely', thought I,
     'This is the lace of Peace's coat;
      I will search out the matter'.   10
But while I looked, the clouds immediately
        Did break and scatter.

Then went I to a garden, and did spy
        A gallant flower,
     The crown imperial: 'Sure', said I,   15
      'Peace at the root must dwell'.
But when I digged, I saw a worm devour
        What showed so well.

At length I met a reverend, good, old man
        Whom, when for Peace   20
     I did demand, he thus began:
      'There was a prince of old
At Salem dwelt, who lived with good increase
        Of flock and fold.

'He sweetly lived; yet sweetness did not save   25
        His life from foes.
     But, after death, out of his grave
      There sprang twelve stalks of wheat,
Which many, wondering at, got some of those
        To plant and set.   30

'It prospered strangely, and did soon disperse
    Through all the earth,
  For they that taste it do rehearse
  That virtue lies therein –
A secret virtue, bringing peace and mirth   35
    By flight of sin.

'Take of this grain, which in my garden grows,
    And grows for you.
  Make bread of it: and that repose
  And peace which everywhere   40
With so much earnestness you do pursue,
    Is only there.'

THOMAS CAREW

The Enquiry

  Amongst the myrtles as I walked,
  Love and my sighs thus intertalked:
  'Tell me' (said I in deep distress)
  'Where may I find my shepherdess?'

  'Thou fool' (said Love), 'know'st thou not this, 5
  In everything that's good she is.
  In yonder tulip go and seek:
  There thou mayest find her lip, her cheek;

  'In yon enamelled pansy by,
  There thou shalt have her curious eye; 10
  In bloom of peach, in rosy bud,
  There wave the streamers of her blood;

  'In brightest lilies that there stands,
  The emblems of her whiter hands;

In yonder rising hill there smells   15
Such sweets as in her bosom dwells.'

''Tis true,' said I, and thereupon
I went to pluck them one by one
To make of parts a union –
But, on a sudden, all was gone.   20

With that I stopped. Said Love: 'These be
(Fond man) resemblances of thee,
And, as these flowers, thy joys shall die
Even in the twinkling of an eye.
   And all thy hopes of her shall wither   25
   Like these short sweets thus knit together.'

JAMES SHIRLEY

The Garden

This garden does not take my eyes,
Though here you show how art of men
Can purchase nature at a price
Would stock old paradise again.

These glories while you dote upon   5
I envy not your spring nor pride –
Nay, boast the summer all your own,
My thoughts with less are satisfied.

Give me a little plot of ground
Where might I with the sun agree;   10
Though every day he walk the round,
My garden he should seldom see.

Those tulips that such wealth display
To court my eye, shall lose their name,
Though now they listen as if they   15
Expected I should praise their flame.

But I would see myself appear
Within the violet's drooping head,
On which a melancholy tear
The discontented morn hath shed.   20

Within their buds let roses sleep,
And virgin lilies on their stem,
Till sighs from lovers glide and creep
Into their leaves to open them.

In the centre of my ground compose   25
Of bays and yew my summer room,
Which may, so oft as I repose,
Present my arbour, and my tomb.

No woman here shall find me out;
Or, if a chance do bring one hither,   30
I'll be secure, for round about
I'll moat it with my eye's foul weather.

No bird shall live within my pale
To charm me with their shames of art,
Unless some wandering nightingale   35
Come here to sing and break her heart,

Upon whose death I'll try to write
An epitaph in some funeral stone
So sad, and true, it may invite
Myself to die, and prove mine own.   40

SIR THOMAS BROWNE (attrib.)

'The almond flourisheth . . .'

The almond flourisheth, the birch trees flow,
The sad mezereon cheerfully doth blow;
The flowery sons before their fathers seen;
The snails begin to crop the mandrake green;
The vernal sun with crocus gardens fills,   5
With hyacinths, anemones and daffodils;
The hazel catkins now dilate and fall,
And paronychions peep upon each wall.

JOHN MILTON

Eden

In narrow room Nature's whole wealth – yea, more,
A heaven on earth; for blissful paradise
Of God the garden was, by him in the east
Of Eden planted. Eden stretched her line
From Auran eastward to the royal towers   5
Of great Seleucia, built by Grecian kings,
Or where the sons of Eden long before
Dwelt in Telassar. In this pleasant soil
His far more pleasant garden God ordained;
Out of the fertile ground he caused to grow   10
All trees of noblest kind for sight, smell, taste;
And all amid them stood the tree of life
High eminent, blooming ambrosial fruit
Of vegetable gold; and, next to life,
Our death, the tree of knowledge, grew fast by –   15
Knowledge of good bought dear by knowing ill.
Southward through Eden went a river large,
Nor changed his course, but through the shaggy hill

Passed underneath, engulfed; for God had thrown
That mountain as his garden mould high raised   20
Upon the rapid current, which, through veins
Of porous earth, with kindly thirst updrawn,
Rose a fresh fountain, and with many a rill
Watered the garden, thence united fell
Down the steep glade, and met the nether flood,   25
Which from his darksome passage now appears
And, now divided into four main streams,
Runs diverse, wandering many a famous realm
And country whereof here needs no account;
But rather to tell how, if art could tell,   30
How from that sapphire fount the crisped brooks,
Rolling on orient pearl and sands of gold,
With mazy error under pendant shades,
Ran nectar, visiting each plant, and fed
Flowers worthy of paradise which not nice art   35
In beds and curious knots, but Nature boon
Poured forth profuse on hill and dale and plain,
Both where the morning sun first warmly smote
The open field, and where the unpierced shade
Embrowned the noontide bowers. Thus was this place   40
A happy rural seat of various view:
Groves whose rich trees wept odorous gums and balm,
Others whose fruit burnished with golden rind
Hung amiable, Hesperian fables true –
If true, here only – and of delicious taste.   45
Betwixt them lawns, or level downs, and flocks
Grazing the tender herb, were interposed,
Or palmy hillock, or the flowery lap
Of some irriguous valley spread her store,
Flowers of all hue, and without thorn the rose.   50
Another side, umbrageous grots and caves
Of cool recess, o'er which the mantling vine
Lays forth her purple grape, and gently creeps
Luxuriant. Meanwhile, murmuring waters fall
Down the slope hills dispersed, or in a lake   55
(That to the fringed bank with myrtle crowned
Her crystal mirror holds) unite their streams.
The birds their choir apply; airs, vernal airs,

Breathing the smell of field and grove, attune
The trembling leaves, while universal Pan   60
Knit with the Graces and the Hours in dance
Led on the eternal spring. . . .

JOSEPH BEAUMONT

The Garden

The garden's quit with me. As yesterday
I walked in that, today that walks in me:
    Through all my memory
It sweetly wanders, and has found a way
    To make me honestly possess   5
      What still another's is.

Yet this gain's dainty sense doth gall my mind
With the remembrance of a bitter loss.
    Alas, how odd and cross
Are earth's delights, in which the soul can find   10
    No honey but withal some sting
      To check the pleasing thing.

For now I'm haunted with the thought of that
    Heaven-planted garden, where felicity
      Flourished on every tree.   15
Lost, lost it is; for at the guarded gate
    A flaming sword forbiddeth sin
      (That's I) to enter in.

O paradise! When I was turned out,
Hadst thou but kept the serpent still within,   20
    My banishment had been
Less sad and dangerous; but round about
    This wide world runneth raging he
      To banish me from me.

I feel that through my soul he death hath shot,   25
And thou, alas, hast locked up life's tree.
    Oh miserable me!
What help were left had Jesus' pity not
  Showed me another tree, which can
    Enliven dying man –   30

That tree, made fertile by his own dear blood,
And by his death with quickening virtue fraught.
    I now dread not the thought
Of barricadoed Eden, since as good
  A paradise I planted see   35
    On open Calvary.

ROWLAND WATKYNS

The Gardener

'She, supposing him to be the gardener,
said unto him' (John 20)

Mary prevents the day: she rose to weep,
And see the bed where Jesus lay asleep.
She found out whom she sought, but doth not know
Her master's face; he is the gardener now.
This gardener Eden's garden did compose,
For which the chiefest plants and flowers he chose;
He took great care to have sweet rivers run
To enrich the ground where he his work begun.
He is the gardener still, and knoweth how
To make the lilies and the roses grow.   10
He knows the time to set, when to remove
His living plants to make them better prove.
He hath his pruning knife, when we grow wild,
To tame our nature, and make us more mild:
He curbs his dearest children; when 'tis need,   15

He cuts his choicest vine and makes it bleed;
He weeds the poisonous herbs which clog the ground;
He knows the rotten hearts, he knows the sound.
The blessed virgin was the pleasant bower
This gardener lodged in his appointed hour: 20
Before his birth his garden was the womb;
In death he in a garden chose his tomb.

ABRAHAM COWLEY

The Wish

    Well then; I now do plainly see
This busy world and I shall ne'er agree;
The very honey of all earthly joy
    Does of all meats the soonest cloy,
    And they (methinks) deserve my pity   5
Who for it can endure the stings,
The crowd, and buzz, and murmurings
    Of this great hive, the city.

    Ah, yet, ere I descend to the grave
May I a small house and large garden have,   10
And a few friends, and many books, both true,
    Both wise, and both delightful too!
    And since love ne'er will from me flee,
A mistress, moderately fair,
And good as guardian angels are,   15
    Only beloved, and loving me!

    O fountains, when in you shall I
Myself, eased of unpeaceful thoughts, espy?
O fields! O woods! When, when shall I be made
    The happy tenant of your shade?   20
    Here's the spring-head of pleasure's flood;
Here's wealthy Nature's treasury,

Where all the riches lie that she
    Has coined and stamped for good.

    Pride and Ambition here   25
Only in far-fetched metaphors appear;
Here nought but winds can hurtful murmurs scatter,
    And nought but Echo flatter.
    The gods, when they descended, hither
From heaven did always choose their way;   30
And therefore we may boldly say,
    That 'tis the way, too, thither.

    How happy here should I
And one dear she live, and, embracing, die!
She who is all the world, and can exclude   35
    In desert's solitude.
    I should have then this only fear,
Lest men, when they my pleasures see,
Should hither throng to live like me,
    And so make a city here.   40

ROBERT HEATH

On Clarastella Walking in Her Garden

    See how Flora smiles to see
    This approaching deity,
    Where each herb looks young and green
    In presence of their coming queen!
    Ceres with all her fragrant store   5
    Could never boast so sweet a flower,
    While thus in triumph she doth go,
    The greater goddess of the two.
        Here the violet bows to greet
    Her with homage to her feet;   10

There the lily pales with white
Got by her reflexed light;
Here a rose in crimson dye
Blushes through her modesty;
There a pansy hangs his head,   15
About to shrink into his bed
Because so quickly she passed by,
Not returning suddenly;
Here the currants, red and white,
In yon green bush, at her sight   20
Peep through the shady leaves and cry
'Come eat me' as she passes by;
There a bed of camomile,
When she presseth it, doth smell
More fragrant than the perfumed east,   25
Or the phoenix' spicy nest;
Here the pinks in rows do throng
To guard her as she walks along;
There the flexive turnsole bends,
Guided by the rays she sends   30
From her bright eyes, as if thence
It sucked life by influence;
Whilst she, the prime and chiefest flower
In all the garden, by her power
And only life-inspiring breath,   35
Like the warm sun redeems from death
Their drooping heads, and bids them live
To tell us she their sweets did give.

ANDREW MARVELL

from **Upon Appleton House:
To My Lord Fairfax**

From that blest bed the hero came
Whom France and Poland yet does fame,
Who, when retired here to peace,
His warlike studies could not cease,
But laid these gardens out in sport   5
In the just figure of a fort,
And with five bastions did it fence
As aiming one for every sense.

When in the east the morning ray
Hangs out the colours of the day,   10
The bee through these known alleys hums,
Beating the dian with its drums.
Then flowers their drowsy eyelids raise,
Their silken ensigns each displays,
And dries its pan yet dank with dew,   15
And fills its flask with odours new.

These, as their governor goes by,
In fragrant volleys they let fly;
And, to salute their governess,
Again as great a charge they press: 20
None for the virgin nymph, for she
Seems with the flowers a flower to be.
And think so still – though not compare
With breadth so sweet or cheek so fair.

Well shot, ye firemen! Oh, how sweet   25
And round your equal fires do meet,
Whose shrill report no ear can tell,
But echoes to the eye and smell.
See how the flowers, as at parade,
Under their colours stand displayed: 30

Each regiment in order grows,
That of the tulip, pink and rose.

But when the vigilant patrol
Of stars walks round about the Pole,
Their leaves, that to the stalks are curled,   35
Seem to their staves the ensigns furled.
Then in some flower's beloved hut
Each bee as sentinel is shut,
And sleeps so, too; but if once stirred,
She runs you through, nor asks the word.   40

O thou, that dear and happy isle,
The garden of the world ere while;
Thou paradise of four seas,
Which heaven planted us to please,
But, to exclude the world, did guard   45
With watery, if not flaming, sword:
What luckless apple did we taste
To make us mortal and thee waste?

Unhappy! shall we never more
That sweet militia restore,   50
When gardens only had their towers,
And all the garrisons were flowers;
When roses only arms might bear,
And men did rosy garlands wear?
Tulips, in several colours barred,   55
Were then the Switzers of our guard.

The gardener had the soldier's place,
And his more gentle forts did trace.
The nursery of all things green
Was then the only magazine.   60
The winter quarters were the stoves
Where he the tender plants removes.
But war all this doth overgrow:
We ordnance plant, and powder sow.

And yet there walks one on the sod   65
Who, had it pleased him and God,
Might once have made our gardens spring
Fresh as his own, and flourishing.
But he preferred to the Cinque Ports
These five imaginary forts,   70
And in those half-dry trenches spanned
Power which the ocean might command.

For he did, with his utmost skill,
Ambition weed but conscience till –
Conscience, that heaven-nursed plant   75
Which most our earthly gardens want.
A prickling leaf it bears, and such
As that which shrinks at every touch,
But flowers eternal and divine
That in the crowns of saints do shine . . .   80

So when the shadows laid asleep
From underneath these banks do creep,
And on the river as it flows
With eben shuts begin to close,
The modest halcyon comes in sight,   85
Flying betwixt the day and night,
And such an horror calm and dumb
Admiring nature does benumb.

The viscous air, wheresoe'er she fly,
Follows and sucks her azure dye;   90
The jellying stream compacts below
If it might fix her shadow so;
The stupid fishes hang, as plain
As flies in crystal o'erta'en;
And men the silent scene assist,   95
Charmed with the sapphire-winged mist.

Maria such, and so doth hush
The world, and through the evening rush.
No new-born comet such a train
Draws through the sky, nor star new-slain;   100

For straight those giddy rockets fail
Which from the putrid earth exhale;
But by her flames, in heaven tried,
Nature is wholly vitrified.

'Tis she that to these gardens gave   105
That wondrous beauty which they have;
She straightness on the woods bestows;
To her the meadow sweetness owes;
Nothing could make the river be
So crystal pure but only she;   110
She yet more pure, sweet, straight and fair
Than gardens, woods, meads, rivers are.

Therefore what first she on them spent
They gratefully again present:
The meadow, carpets where to tread;   115
The garden, flowers to crown her head;
And, for a glass, the limpid brook,
Where she may all her beauties look;
But, since she would not have them seen,
The wood about her draws a screen . . .   120

The Garden

How vainly men themselves amaze
To win the palm, the oak, or bays,
And their uncessant labours see
Crowned from some single herb or tree
Whose short and narrow vergèd shade   5
Does prudently their toils upbraid,
While all flowers and all trees do close
To weave the garlands of repose.

Fair Quiet, have I found thee here,
And Innocence, thy sister dear?   10
Mistaken long, I sought you then

In busy companies of men –
Your sacred plants, if here below,
Only among the plants will grow:
Society is all but rude   15
To this delicious solitude.

No white nor red was ever seen
So amorous as this lovely green.
Fond lovers, cruel as their flame,
Cut in these trees their mistress' name –   20
Little, alas, they know, or heed,
How far these beauties hers exceed.
Fair trees, wheresoe'er your barks I wound,
No name shall but your own be found.

When we have run our passion's heat,   25
Love hither makes his best retreat.
The gods, that mortal beauty chase,
Still in a tree did end their race:
Apollo hunted Daphne so
Only that she might laurel grow,   30
And Pan did after Syrinx speed
Not as a nymph, but for a reed.

What wondrous life is this I lead!
Ripe apples drop about my head;
The luscious clusters of the vine   35
Upon my mouth do crush their wine;
The nectarine and curious peach
Into my hands themselves do reach;
Stumbling on melons as I pass,
Ensnared with flowers, I fall on grass.   40

Meanwhile the mind, from pleasures less,
Withdraws into its happiness:
The mind – that ocean where each kind
Does straight his own resemblance find.
Yet it creates – transcending these –   45
Far other worlds, and other seas,
Annihilating all that's made
To a green thought in a green shade.

Here, at the fountain's sliding foot,
Or at some fruit tree's mossy root,   50
Casting the body's vest aside,
My soul into the boughs does glide:
There, like a bird, it sits and sings,
Then whets and combs its silver wings,
And, till prepared for longer flight,   55
Waves in its plumes the various light.

Such was that happy garden state
While man there walked without a mate:
After a place so pure and sweet,
What other help could yet be meet!   60
But 'twas beyond a mortal's share
To wander solitary there –
Two paradises 'twere in one
To live in paradise alone.

How well the skilful gardener drew   65
Of flowers and herbs this dial new,
Where, from above, the milder sun
Does through a fragrant zodiac run,
And, as it works, the industrious bee
Computes its time as well as we!   70
How could such sweet and wholesome hours
Be reckoned but with herbs and flowers!

The Mower against Gardens

Luxurious man, to bring his vice in use,
    Did after him the world seduce,
And from the fields the flowers and plants allure
    Where nature was most plain and pure.
He first enclosed within the gardens square   5
    A dead and standing pool of air,

And a more luscious earth for them did knead,
    Which stupefied them while it fed.
The pink grew then as double as his mind –
    The nutriment did change the kind.   10
With strange perfumes he did the roses taint,
    And flowers themselves were taught to paint;
The tulip – white – did for complexion seek,
    And learned to interline its cheek:
Its onion root they then so high did hold   15
    That one was for a meadow sold.
Another world was searched, through oceans new,
    To find the 'Marvel of Peru'.
And yet these rarities might be allowed
    To man – that sovereign thing and proud –   20
Had he not dealt, between the bark and tree,
    Forbidden mixtures there to see.
No plant now knew the stock from which it came;
    He grafts upon the wild the tame,
That the uncertain and adulterate fruit   25
    Might put the palate in dispute.
His green seraglio has its eunuchs, too
    (Lest any tyrant him outdo),
And in the cherry he does nature vex
    To procreate without a sex.   30
'Tis all enforced, the fountain and the grot,
    While the sweet fields do lie forgot,
Where willing nature does to all dispense
    A wild and fragrant innocence,
And fauns and fairies do the meadows till   35
    More by their presence than their skill.
Their statues, polished by some ancient hand,
    May, to adorn the gardens, stand:
But, howsoe'er the figures do excel,
    The gods themselves with us do dwell.   40

HENRY VAUGHAN

Regeneration

A ward, and still in bonds, one day
        I stole abroad:
It was high spring, and all the way
        Primrosed, and hung with shade;
          Yet it was frost within,   5
          And surly winds
Blasted my infant buds, and sin
        Like clouds eclipsed my mind.

Stormed thus, I straight perceived my spring
        Mere stage and show,   10
My walk a monstrous, mountained thing
        Rough-cast with rocks and snow;
          And, as a pilgrim's eye,
          Far from relief,
Measures the melancholy sky   15
        Then drops, and rains for grief,

So sighed I upwards still. At last,
        'Twixt steps and falls,
I reached the pinnacle, where placed
        I found a pair of scales.   20
        I took them up and laid
        In the one late pains,
The other smoke and pleasures weighed,
        But proved the heavier grains.

With that, some cried 'Away'; straight I   25
        Obeyed and, led
Full east, a fair, fresh field could spy.
        Some called it 'Jacob's bed' –
        A virgin soil, which no
          Rude feet ere trod,   30
Where (since he stepped there) only go
        Prophets and friends of God.

Here I reposed; but, scarce well-set,
    A grove descried
Of stately height, whose branches met   35
    And mixed on every side.
    I entered, and once in
        (Amazed to see it)
Found all was changed, and a new spring
    Did all my senses greet.   40

The unthrift sun shot vital gold –
    A thousand pieces –
And heaven its azure did unfold
    Chequered with snowy fleeces.
    The air was all in spice,   45
    And every bush
A garland wore. Thus fed my eyes,
    But all the ear lay hush.

Only a little fountain lent
    Some use for ears,   50
And on the dumb shades Language spent
    The music of her tears;
    I drew her near, and found
    The cistern full
Of diverse stones, some bright and round,   55
    Others ill-shaped and dull.

The first (pray mark) as quick as light
    Danced through the flood;
But the last, more heavy than the night,
    Nailed to the centre stood.   60
    I wondered much; but, tired
    At last with thought,
My restless eye, that still desired,
    As strange an object brought.

It was a bank of flowers, where I descried   65
    (Though 'twas midday)
Some fast asleep, others broad-eyed
    And taking in the ray.

> Here musing long, I heard
> A rushing wind   70
Which still increased, but whence it stirred
> Nowhere I could not find.

> I turned me round, and to each shade
> Dispatched an eye
To see if any leaf had made   75
> Least motion or reply;
> But while I, listening, sought
> My mind to ease
By knowing where 'twas, or where not,
> It whispered, 'Where I please'.   80

> 'Lord', then said I, 'on me one breath,
> And let me die before my death'.

Song of Solomon, 4:16
Arise, O north, and come, thou south wind, and blow upon my garden,
that the spices thereof may blow out.

MARGARET CAVENDISH

A Landscape

Standing upon a hill of fancies high,
Viewing about with curiosity's eye,
Saw several landscapes under my thoughts to lie.
  Some champians of delights where there did feed
Pleasures, as wethers fat, and ewes to breed;   5
And pastures of green hopes, wherein cows went,
Of probability give milk of sweet content.
Some fields, though ploughed with care, unsowed did lie,
Wanting the fruitful seed, industry.
In other fields full crops of joys there growed,   10
Where some ripe joy's fruition down had mowed.

Some, blasted with ill accidents, looked black;
Others, blown down with sorrow strong, lay flat.
    Then did I view enclosures close to lie,
Hearts hedged about with thoughts of secrecy.   15
Fresh meadow of green youth did pleasant seem:
Innocency, as cowslips, grew therein;
Some ready with old age to cut for hay,
Some hay cocked high for death to take away;
Clear rivulets of health ran here and there: 20
No mind of sickness in them did appear,
No stones or gravel stopped their passage free,
No weeds of pain or slimy gouts could see.
    Woods did present my view on the left side,
Where trees of high ambition grew great pride: 25
There shades of envy were made of dark spite,
Which did eclipse the fame of honour's light.
Faults stood so close not many beams of praise
Could enter in: spite stopped up all the ways.
But leaves of prattling tongues, which ne'er lie still,   30
Sometimes speak truth, although most lies they tell.
    Then did I a garden of beauty view,
Where complexions of roses and lilies grew;
And violets of blue veins there growed,
Upon the banks of breasts most perfect showed;   35
Lips of fresh gillyflowers grew up high,
Which oft the sun did kiss as he passed by;
Hands of Narcissus perfect white were set;
The palms were curious tulips, finely streaked.
    And by this garden a lovely orchard stood,   40
Wherein grew fruit of pleasure rare and good.
All coloured eyes grew there, as bullace grey,
And damsons black (which do taste best, some say).
Others there were of the pure bluest grape,
And pear-plum faces of an oval shape,   45
Cheeks of apricots made red with heat,
And cherry lips, which most delight to eat.
When I had viewed this landscape round about,
I fell from Fancy's hill, and so wit's sight went out.

N. HOOKES

To Amanda Walking in the Garden

And now what monarch would not gardener be,
My fair Amanda's stately gait to see?
How her feet tempt! How swift and light she treads,
Fearing to wake the flowers from their beds!
Yet from their sweet green pillows everywhere   5
They start and gaze about to see my fair.
Look at yon flower yonder, how it grows,
Sensibly! How it opes its leaves and blows,
Puts its best Easter clothes on, neat and gay:
Amanda's presence makes it holiday!   10
Look how, on tiptoe, that fair lily stands
To look on thee, and court thy whiter hands
To gather it. I saw in yonder crowd –
That tulip bed of which Dame Flora's proud –
A short dwarf flower did enlarge its stalk,   15
And shoot an inch to see Amanda walk.
Nay, look, my fairest – look how fast they grow,
Into a scaffold-method spring, as though,
Riding to Parliament, were to be seen
In pomp and state some royal amorous queen.   20
The gravelled walks, though even as a die,
Lest some loose pebble should offensive lie,
Quilt themselves o'er with downy moss for thee.
The walls are hanged with blossomed tapestry
To hide their nakedness when looked upon;   25
The maiden fig-tree puts Eve's apron on;
The broad-leaved sycamore, and every tree,
Shakes like a trembling asp, and bends to thee,
And each leaf proudly strives with fresher air
To fan the curled tresses of thy hair.   30
Nay, and the bee, too, with his wealthy thigh,
Mistakes his hive and to thy lips doth fly,
Willing to treasure up his honey there,
Where honeycombs so sweet and plenty are.
Look how that pretty, modest columbine   35

Hangs down its head to view those feet of thine;
See the fond motion of the strawberry
Creeping on the earth to go along with thee!
The lovely violet makes after, too,
Unwilling yet, my dear, to part with you;   40
The knot-grass and the daisies catch thy toes
To kiss my fair one's feet before she goes.
All court and wish me lay Amanda down,
And give my dear a new green-flowered gown.
   Come, let me kiss thee falling, kiss at rise,   45
   Thou in the garden, I in paradise.

CHARLES COTTON

Chatsworth

Upon a terrace, as most houses high
(Though from this prospect humble to your eye),
A stately plat, both regular and vast,
Suiting the rest, was by the foundress cast
In those incurious times, under the rose,   5
Designed – as one may saucily suppose –
For lilies, peonies, daffodils and roses
To garnish chimneys and make Sunday posies,
Where gooseberries, as good as ever grew,
'Tis like were set; for winter-greens, the yew,   10
Holly, and box – for then these things were new –
With oh! the honest rosemary and bays,
So much esteemed in those good wassail days.
   Now in the middle of this great parterre
A fountain darts her streams into the air   15
Twenty foot high, till, by the winds depressed,
Unable longer upward to contest,
They fall again in tears of grief and ire
They cannot reach the place they did aspire:
As if the sun melted the waxen wings   20

Of these Icarian temerarious springs
For braving thus his generative ray,
When their true motion lies another way.
The ambitious element, repulsed so,
Rallies, and saves her routed waves below   25
In a large basin of diameter
Such as old Rome's expansive lakes did bear,
Where a Pacific sea expanded lies,
A liquid theatre for naumachies,
And where, in case of such a pageant war,   30
Romans in statue still spectators are. . . .

ALEXANDER POPE

The Gardens of Alcinous
from the Seventh Book of Homer's Odysses

Close to the gates a spacious garden lies,
From storms defended, and inclement skies:
Four acres was the allotted space of ground,
Fenced with a green enclosure all around.
Tall, thriving trees confessed the fruitful mould;   5
The reddening apple ripens here to gold;
Here the blue fig with luscious juice o'erflows;
With deeper red the full pomegranate glows;
The branch here bends beneath the weighty pear,
And verdant olives flourish round the year.   10
The balmy spirit of the western gale
Eternal breathes on fruit untaught to fail:
Each dropping pear a following pear supplies,
On apples apples, figs on figs arise:
The same mild season gives the blooms to blow,   15
The buds to harden, and the fruits to grow.
    Here ordered vines in equal ranks appear
With all the united labours of the year:

Some to unload the fertile branches run;
Some dry the blackening clusters in the sun;   20
Others to tread the liquid harvest join:
The groaning presses foam with floods of wine.
Here are the vines in early flower descried,
Here grapes discoloured on the sunny side,
And there in autumn's richest purple dyed.   25
Beds of all various herbs, forever green,
In beauteous order terminate the scene.
    Two plenteous fountains the whole prospect crowned:
This through the gardens leads its streams around,
Visits each plant, and waters all the ground;   30
While that in pipes beneath the palace flows,
And thence its current on the town bestows:
To various use their various streams they bring,
The people one, and one supplies the king.

from Moral Essay 4,
The Epistle to Burlington

    To build, to plant – whatever you intend –
To rear the column, or the arch to bend,
To swell the terrace, or to sink the grot,
In all let Nature never be forgot,
But treat the goddess like a modest fair,   5
Nor over-dress, nor leave her wholly bare:
Let not each beauty everywhere be spied,
Where half the skill is decently to hide.
He gains all points who pleasingly confounds,
Surprises, varies, and conceals the bounds.   10
    Consult the Genius of the Place in all:
That tells the waters or to rise or fall,
Or helps the ambitious hill the heaven to scale,
Or scoops in circling theatres the vale,
Calls in the country, catches opening glades,   15

Joins willing woods, and varies shades from shades;
Now breaks or now directs the intending lines,
Paints as you plant and, as you work, designs.
    Still follow sense, of every art the soul,
Parts answering parts shall slide into a whole,   20
Spontaneous beauties all around advance,
Start even from difficulty, strike from chance:
Nature shall join you, Time shall make it grow
A work to wonder at – perhaps a Stowe.
    Without it, proud Versailles, thy glory falls,   25
And Nero's terraces desert their walls . . .
    At Timon's villa let us pass a day,
Where all cry out 'What sums are thrown away!'
So proud, so grand, of that stupendous air,
Soft and agreeable come never there.   30
Greatness, with Timon, dwells in such a draught
As brings all Brobdingnag before your thought.
To compass this his building is a town,
His pond an ocean, his parterre a down:
Who but must laugh the master when he sees,   35
A puny insect, shivering at a breeze!
Lo, what huge heaps of littleness around –
The whole, a laboured quarry above ground.
Two Cupids squirt before; a lake behind
Improves the keenness of the northern wind.   40
His gardens next your admiration call:
On every side you look, behold, the wall!
No pleasing intricacies intervene,
No artful wildness to perplex the scene:
Grove nods at grove, each alley has a brother,   45
And half the platform just reflects the other.
The suffering eye inverted nature sees –
Trees cut to statues, statues thick as trees,
With here a fountain never to be played,
And there a summer house that knows no shade;   50
Here Amphitrite sails through myrtle bowers;
There gladiators fight, or die, in flowers.
Unwatered see the drooping sea-horse mourn,
And swallows roost in Nilus' dusty urn.

JAMES THOMSON

The Seasons; from Spring

These are the sacred feelings of thy heart,
Thy heart informed by reason's purer ray,
O Lyttleton, the friend! Thy passions thus
And meditations vary, as at large,
Courting the Muse, through Hagley Park you stray,
Thy British Tempe. There along the dale   5
With woods o'erhung, and shagged with mossy rocks
Whence on each hand the gushing waters play,
And down the rough cascade white-dashing fall
Or gleam in lengthened vista through the trees,
You silent steal; or sit beneath the shade   10
Of solemn oaks that tuft the swelling mounts
Thrown graceful round by Nature's careless hand,
And pensive listen to the various voice
Of rural peace – the herds, the flocks, the birds,
The hollow-whispering breeze, the plaint of rills   15
That, purling down amid the twisted roots
Which creep around, their dewy murmurs shake
On the soothed ear. From these abstracted oft,
You wander through the philosophic world
Where, in bright train, continual wonders rise   20
Or to the curious or the pious eye . . .
Meantime you gain the height, from whose fair brow
The bursting prospect spreads immense around;
And, snatched o'er hill and dale, and wood and lawn,
And verdant field, and darkening heath between,   25
And villages enbosomed soft in trees,
And spiry towns by surging columns marked
Of household smoke, your eye excursive roams –
Wide-stretching from the Hall in whose kind haunt
The hospitable Genius lingers still,   30
To where the broken landscape, by degrees
Ascending, roughens into rigid hills
O'er which the Cambrian mountains, like far clouds
That skirt the blue horizon, dusky rise . . .

WILLIAM SHENSTONE

from **The Schoolmistress**

Herbs, too, she knew, and well of each could speak,
That in her garden sipped the silvery dew,
Where no vain flower disclosed a gaudy streak,
But herbs for use and physic – not a few –
Of grey renown within those borders grew: 5
The tufted basil; pun-provoking thyme;
Fresh balm; and marigold of cheerful hue;
The lowly gill, that never dares to climb,
And more I fain would sing, disdaining here to rhyme.

Yet euphrasy may not be left unsung,   10
That gives dim eyes to wander leagues around;
And pungent radish, biting infant's tongue;
And plaintain ribbed, that heals the reaper's wound;
And marjoram sweet, in shepherd's posy found;
And lavender, whose spikes of azure bloom   15
Shall be, erewhile, in arid bundles bound,
To hang amidst the labours of her loom,
And crown her kerchiefs clean with mickle pure perfume.

And here trim rosemarine, that whilom crowned
The daintiest garden of the proudest peer   20
Ere, driven from its envied site, it found
A sacred shelter for its branches here,
Where, edged with gold, its glittering skirts appear.
O wassail days, O customs meet and well
Ere this was banished from its lofty sphere;   25
Simplicity then sought this humble cell,
Nor ever would she more with thane and lordling dwell . . .

WILLIAM MASON

from **The English Garden, Book III**

Lured by their hasty shoots and branching stems,
Planters there are who choose the race of pine
For this great end, erroneous: witless they
That, as their arrowy heads assault the sky,
They leave their shafts unfeathered. Rather, thou   5
Select the shrubs that, patient of the knife,
Will thank thee for the wound: the hardy thorn,
Holly, or box, privet or pyracanth.
They, thickening from their base, with tenfold shade
Will soon replenish all thy judgement pruned.   10
  But chief, with willing aid, her glittering green
Shall England's laurels bring: swift shall she spread
Her broad-leaved shade, and float it fair and wide,
Proud to be called an inmate of the soil.
Let England prize this daughter of the East   15
Beyond that Latian plant, of kindred name,
That wreathed the head of Julius, basely twined
Its flattering foliage on the traitor's brow
Who crushed his country's freedom. Sacred tree,
Ne'er be thy brighter verdure thus debased!   20
Far happier thou, in this sequestered bower,
To shroud thy poet, who, with fostering hand,
Here bade thee flourish, and with grateful strain
Now chants the praise of thy maturer bloom . . .
  Nor are the plants which England calls her own   25
Few, or unlovely, that, with laurel joined,
And kindred foliage of perennial green,
Will form a close-knit curtain. Shrubs there are
Of bolder growth, that, at the call of spring,
Burst forth in blossomed fragrance: lilacs robed   30
In snow-white innocence or purple pride;
The sweet syringa yielding but in scent
To the rich orange; or the woodbine mild
That loves to hang, on barren boughs remote,
Her wreaths of flowery perfume. . . .   35

What next we from the Dryad powers implore
Is grace, is ornament: for see! our lawn,
Though clothed with softest verdure, though relieved
By many a gentle and easy swell,
Expects that harmony of light and shade   40
Which foliage only gives. Come then, ye plants,
That, like the village troop when Maia dawns,
Delight to mingle social. To the crest
Of yonder brow we safely may conduct
Your numerous train. No eye obstructed here   45
Will blame your interposed society,
But, on the plain below, in single stems
Disparted, or in sparing groups distinct,
Wide must ye stand, in wild disordered mood,
As if the seeds from which your scions sprang   50
Had there been scattered from the affrighted beak
Of some maternal bird whom the fierce hawk
Pursued with felon claw. . . .
Far to the north of thy imperial towers,
Augusta, in that wild and alpine vale   55
Through which the Swale, by mountain torrents swelled,
Flings his redundant stream, there lived a youth
Of polished manners. Ample his domain,
And fair the site of his paternal dome.
He loved the art I sing: a deep adept   60
In Nature's story, well he knew the names
Of all her verdant lineage. Yet that skill
Missed his taste. Scornful of every bloom
That spreads spontaneous, from remotest Ind
He brought his foliage, careless of its cost,   65
Even of its beauty careless: it was rare,
And therefore beauteous. Now his laurel screen,
With rose and woodbine negligently wove,
Bows to the axe: the rich magnolias claim
The station. Now Herculean beeches, felled,   70
Resign their rights, and warm Virginia sends
Her cedars to usurp them. The proud oak
Himself – even he, the sovereign of the shade –
Yields to the fir that drips with Gilead's balm.
Now Albion gaze at glories not thy own!   75

Pause, rapid Swale, and see thy margin crowned
With all the pride of Ganges: vernal showers
Have fixed their roots; nutritious summer suns
Favoured their growth; and mildest autumn smiled
Benignant o'er them. Vigorous, fair and tall,   80
They waft a gale of spices o'er the plain.
But winter comes, and with him watery Jove,
And with him Boreas in his frozen shroud.
The savage spirit of old Swale is roused;
He howls amidst his foam. At the dread sight   85
The alien stand aghast; they bow their heads.
In vain the glassy penthouse is supplied:
The pelting storm with icy bullets breaks
Its fragile barrier: see! they fade, they die!

WILLIAM COWPER

from The Task, Book III

Who loves a garden loves a greenhouse, too.
Unconscious of a less propitious clime,
There blooms exotic beauty, warm and snug,
While the winds whistle and the snows descend.
The spiry myrtle with unwithering leaf   5
Shines there and flourishes. The golden boast
Of Portugal and western India there,
The ruddier orange, and the paler lime,
Peep through their polished foliage at the storm,
And seem to smile at what they need not fear.   10
The amomum there with intermingling flowers
And cherries hangs her twigs. Geranium boasts
Her crimson honours, and the spangled beau,
Ficoides, glitters bright the winter long.
All plants, of every leaf, that can endure   15
The winter's frown, if screened from his shrewd bite,
Live there and prosper. Those Ausonia claims,

Levantine regions these; the Azores send
Their jessamine, her jessamine remote
Caffraia: foreigners from many lands,   20
They form one social shade, as if convened
By magic summons of the Orphean lyre. . . .
                              Lo, he comes!
The omnipotent magician, Brown, appears!
Down falls the venerable pile, the abode
Of our forefathers – a grave, whiskered race,   25
But tasteless. Springs a palace in its stead,
But in a distant spot where, more exposed,
It may enjoy the advantage of the north
And aguish east, till time shall have transformed
Those naked acres to a sheltering grove.   30
He speaks: the lake in front becomes a lawn;
Woods vanish; hills subside; and valleys rise.
And streams – as if created for his use –
Pursue the track of his directing wand,
Sinuous or straight, now rapid and now slow,   35
Now murmuring soft, now roaring in cascades,
Even as he bids. The enraptured owner smiles. . . .

SUSAN BLAMIRE

'When Home We Return . . .'

When home we return, after youth has been spending,
And many a slow year has been wasting and ending,
We often seem lost in the once well-known places,
And sigh to find age has so furrowed dear faces:
For the rose that has faded the eye still keeps mourning,   5
And weeps every change that it sees on returning.

Should we miss but a tree where we used to be playing,
Or find the wood cut where we sauntered a-Maying –
If the yew seat's away, or the ivy's a-wanting,

We hate the fine lawn and the new-fashioned planting: 10
Each thing called improvement seems blackened with crimes
If it tears up one record of blissful old times.

When many a spring has called forth the sweet flowers,
And many an autumn had painted the bowers,
I came to the place where life had its beginning,   15
Taking root with the groves that around me were springing:
When I found them all gone 'twas like dear friends departed,
And I walked where they used to be, half broken-hearted.

When distant, one bower my fancy still haunted –
'Twas hung round with woodbine my Jessy had planted –   20
I ran to the spot, where a weak flower remaining
Could just nod its head to approve my complaining:
A tear from a dewdrop I hid in its fringes,
And sighed then to think what one's pleasures unhinges.

But, ah! what is that to the friends oft estranging,   25
Their manners still more than their looks daily changing:
Where the heart used to *warm* to find *civil* behaviour,
Makes us wish we had stayed from our country for ever,
With the sweet days of youth in our fancies still glowing,
And the love of old friends with old Time ever growing!   30

WILLIAM BLAKE

To Autumn

O Autumn, laden with fruit, and stained
With the blood of the grape, pass not, but sit
Beneath my shady roof: there thou mayest rest
And tune thy jolly voice to my fresh pipe,
And all the daughters of the year shall dance.   5
Sing now the lusty songs of fruits and flowers.

'The narrow bud opens her beauties to
The sun, and love runs in her thrilling veins;
Blossoms hang round the brows of morning, and
Flourish down the bright cheek of modest eve   10
Till clustering Summer breaks forth into singing,
And feathered clouds strew flowers round her head.

'The spirits of the air live on in smells
Of fruit; and Joy, with pinions light, roves round
The gardens, or sits singing in the trees.'   15
Thus sang the jolly Autumn as he sat;
Then rose, girded himself, and o'er the bleak
Hills fled from our sight; but left his golden load.

from **Milton, Book II**

Thou hearest the nightingale begin the song of spring;
The lark, sitting upon his earthy bed, just as the morn
Appears, listens silent, then, springing from the waving cornfield,
    loud
He leads the choir of day – trill, trill, trill, trill –
Mounting upon the wings of light into the great expanse,   5
Re-echoing against the lovely blue and shining heavenly shell.
His little throat labours with inspiration; every feather
On throat and breast and wings vibrates with the effluence
    divine:
All nature listens silent to him, and the awful Sun
Stands still upon the mountain looking on this little bird   10
With eyes of soft humility, and wonder, love, and awe.
Then loud from their green covert all the birds begin their song.
The thrush, the linnet, and the goldfinch, robin and the wren
Awake the Sun from his sweet reverie upon the mountain:
The nightingale again assays his song, and through the day   15
And through the night warbles luxuriant, every bird of song
Attending his loud harmony with admiration and love.
This is a vision of the lamentation of Beulah over Ololon!

Thou perceivest the flowers put forth their precious odours,
And none can tell how from so small a centre comes such
    sweets,   20
Forgetting that within that centre eternity expands
Its ever-during doors that Og and Anak fiercely guard.
First ere the morning breaks, joy opens in the flowery bosoms,
Joy even to tears, which the Sun rising dries. First, the wild
    thyme
And meadow-sweet downy and soft, waving among the reeds, 25
Light springing on the air, lead the sweet dance: they wake
The honeysuckle sleeping on the oak: the flaunting beauty
Revels along upon the wind; the whitethorn, lovely May,
Opens her many lovely eyes; listening, the rose still sleeps –
None dare to wake her. Soon she bursts her crimson-curtained
    bed   30
And comes forth in the majesty of beauty; every flower –
The pink, the jessamine, the wallflower, the carnation,
The jonquil, the mild lily – opes her heavens! Every tree,
And flower, and herb soon fill the air with an innumerable
    dance,
Yet all in order sweet and lovely. Men are sick with love.   35
Such is a vision of the lamentation of Beulah over Ololon.

WILLIAM WORDSWORTH

A Flower Garden

At Coleorton Hall, Leicestershire

Tell me, ye zephyrs, that unfold,
While fluttering o'er this gay recess,
Pinions that fanned the teeming mould
Of Eden's blissful wilderness,
Did only softly stealing hours   5
There close the peaceful lives of flowers?

Say, when the *moving* creatures saw
All kinds commingled without fear,
Prevailed a like indulgent law
For the still growths that prosper here?   10
Did wanton fawn and kid forbear
The half-blown rose, the lily spare?

Or peeped they often from their beds
And prematurely disappeared,
Devoured like pleasure ere it spreads   15
A bosom to the sun endeared?
If such their harsh untimely doom,
It falls not *here* on bud or bloom.

All summer long the happy Eve
Of this fair spot her flowers may bind,   20
Nor e'er, with ruffled fancy, grieve,
From the next glance she casts, to find
That love for little things by Fate
Is rendered vain as love for great.

Yet, where the guardian fence is wound,   25
So subtly are our eyes beguiled,
We see not nor suspect a bound,
No more than in some forest wild;
The site is free as air – or crossed
Only by art in nature lost.   30

And though the jealous turf refuse
By random footsteps to be pressed,
And feed on never-sullied dews,
Ye, gentle breezes from the west,
With all the ministers of hope   35
Are tempted to this sunny slope!

And hither throngs of birds resort;
Some, inmates lodged in shady nests,
Some, perched on stems of stately port

That nod to welcome transient guests;   40
While hare and leveret, seen at play,
Appear not more shut out than they.

Apt emblem (for reproof of pride)
This delicate enclosure shows
Of modest kindness, that would hide   45
The firm protection she bestows;
Of manners, like its viewless fence,
Ensuring peace to innocence.

Thus spake the moral Muse – her wing
Abruptly spreading to depart,   50
She left that farewell offering,
Memento for some docile heart;
That may respect the good old age
When Fancy was Truth's willing page,
And Truth would skim the flowery glade,   55
Though entering but as Fancy's shade.

'This Lawn, a Carpet all Alive . . .'

This lawn, a carpet all alive
With shadows flung from leaves – to strive
   In dance, amid a press
Of sunshine, an apt emblem yields
Of worldlings revelling in the fields   5
   Of strenuous idleness;

Less quick, the stir when tide and breeze
Encounter, and to narrow seas
   Forbid a moment's rest;
The medley less when boreal lights   10
Glance to and fro, like airy sprites
   To feats of arms addressed!

Yet spite of all this eager strife,
This ceaseless play, the genuine life
    That serves the steadfast hours,   15
Is in the grass beneath, that grows
Unheeded, and the mute repose
Of sweetly-breathing flowers.

SAMUEL TAYLOR COLERIDGE

Reflections on Having Left a Place of Retirement

Low was our pretty cot: our tallest rose
Peeped at the chamber-window. We could hear
At silent noon, and eve, and early morn,
The sea's faint murmur. In the open air
Our myrtles blossomed, and across the porch   5
Thick jasmines twined: the little landscape round
Was green and woody, and refreshed the eye.
It was a spot which you might aptly call
The Valley of Seclusion. Once I saw
(Hallowing his sabbath day by quietness)   10
A wealthy son of commerce saunter by,
Bristowa's citizen: methought it calmed
His thirst of idle gold, and made him muse
With wiser feelings; for he paused, and looked
With a pleased sadness, and gazed all around,   15
Then eyed our cottage, and gazed round again,
And sighed, and said, it was a blessed place.
And we *were* blessed. Oft with patient ear
Long-listening to the viewless skylark's note
(Viewless, or haply for a moment seen   20
Gleaming on sunny wings) in whispered tones

I've said to my beloved: 'Such, sweet girl,
The inobtrusive song of happiness –
Unearthly minstrelsy! Then only heard
When the soul seeks to hear; when all is hushed, 25
And the heart listens!'
                But the time, when first
From that low dell steep up the stony mount
I climbed with perilous toil, and reached the top!
Oh, what a goodly scene! *Here* the bleak mount –
The bare bleak mountain, speckled thin with sheep; 30
Grey clouds that shadowing spot the sunny fields;
And river, now with bushy rocks o'er-browed,
Now winding bright and full, with naked banks;
And seats, and lawns, the abbey and the wood,
And cots and hamlets, and faint city spire; 35
The Channel *there*, the islands and white sails,
Dim coasts and cloud-like hills, and shoreless ocean –
It seemed like omnipresence! God, methought,
Had built him there a temple: the whole world
Seemed *imaged* in its vast circumference: 40
No *wish* profaned my overwhelmed heart.
Blessed hour! It was a luxury, – to be.
   Ah, quiet dell, dear cot, and mount sublime!
I was constrained to quit you. Was it right,
While my unnumbered brethren toiled and bled, 45
That I should dream away the entrusted hours
On rose-leaf beds; pampering the coward heart
With feelings all too delicate for use?
Sweet is the tear that from some Howard's eye
Drops on the cheek of one he lifts from earth: 50
And he that works me good with unmoved face
Does it but half: he chills me while he aids,
My benefactor, not my brother man!
Yet even this, this cold beneficence
Praise, praise it, O my soul, oft as thou scannest 55
The sluggard Pity's vision-weaving tribe,
Who sigh for wretchedness, yet shun the wretched,
Nursing in some delicious solitude
Their slothful loves and dainty sympathies.
I therefore go, and join head, heart, and hand, 60

Active and firm, to fight the bloodless fight
Of Science, Freedom, and the Truth in Christ.
    Yet oft when, after honourable toil,
Rests the tired mind, and waking loves to dream,
My spirit shall revisit thee, dear cot –   65
Thy jasmine and thy window-peeping rose,
And myrtles fearless of the mild sea air.
And I shall sigh fond wishes – sweet abode!
Ah – had none greater! And that all had such!
It might be so – but the time is not yet.   70
    Speed it, O Father. Let thy kingdom come!

THOMAS MOORE

''Tis the Last Rose of Summer'

'Tis the last rose of summer
Left blooming alone:
All her lovely companions
Are faded and gone!
No flower of her kindred,   5
No rosebud is nigh
To reflect back her blushes
Or give sigh for sigh.

I'll not leave thee, thou lone one,
To pine on the stem: 10
Since the lovely are sleeping,
Go, sleep thou with them.
Thus fondly I scatter
Thy leaves o'er the bed
Where thy mates of the garden   15
Lie scentless and dead.

So, soon may I follow
When friendships decay,

And from love's shining circle
The gems drop away.   20
When true hearts lie withered
And fond ones are flown,
Oh, who would inhabit
This bleak world alone?

JOHN KEATS

from 'I Stood Tip-toe Upon a Little Hill'

A bush of May flowers with the bees about them –
Ah, sure no tasteful nook would be without them –
And let a lush laburnum oversweep them,
And let long grass grow round the roots to keep them
Moist, cool and green; and shade the violets,   5
That they may bind the moss in leafy nets.

A filbert hedge with wild briar overtwined,
And clumps of woodbine taking the soft wind
Upon their summer thrones; there too should be
The frequent chequer of a youngling tree,   10
That, with a score of light green brethren, shoots
From the quaint mossiness of aged roots,
Round which is heard a spring-head of clear waters
Babbling so wildly of its lovely daughters,
The spreading bluebells: it may haply mourn
That such fair clusters should be rudely torn   15
From their fresh beds, and scattered thoughtlessly
By infant hands, left on the path to die.
Open afresh your round of starry folds,
Ye ardent marigolds!
Dry up the moisture from your golden lids,   20
For great Apollo bids
That in these days your praises should be sung
On many harps, which he has lately strung.

And when again your dewiness he kisses,
Tell him I have you in my world of blisses,   25
So haply when I rove in some far vale,
His mighty voice may come upon the gale.

Here are sweet peas, on tip-toe for a flight,
With wings of gentle flush o'er delicate white,
And taper fingers catching at all things   30
To bind them all about with tiny rings. . . .

from **The Fall of Hyperion, Canto 1**

Methought I stood where trees of every clime,
Palm, myrtle, oak, and sycamore, and beech,
With plantain, and spice-blossoms, made a screen –
In neighbourhood of fountains, by the noise
Soft-showering in my ears, and, by the touch   5
Of scent, not far from roses. Turning round,
I saw an arbour with a drooping roof
Of trellis vines, and bells, and larger blooms,
Like floral censers swinging light in air;
Before its wreathed doorway, on a mound   10
Of moss, was spread a feast of summer fruits,
Which, nearer seen, seemed refuse of a meal
By angel tasted, or our Mother Eve;
For empty shells were scattered on the grass,
And grape-stalks but half bare, and remnants more,   15
Sweet-smelling, whose pure kinds I could not know . . .

WILLIAM BARNES

The Old Garden (Two sisters, A and B)

(A) How much this garden has lost,
        And kept, of all we long had known,
    Its wall is sound, and on the ground
        Still reaches on this walk of stone;
    And there's the cypress, bending slim,   5
    Beside the spring with rocky brim.

(B) We miss, indeed, some flowers we knew,
        Along the wall, or winding walks;
    The rose, the stocks, and hollyhocks,
        And milk-white pinks, with grey-blue stalks;   10
    But still the walnut-tree o'erspreads
    The ground where once it screened our heads.

(A) These box-bushes that once we trimmed
        Like table-tops, or tipped like spears,
    Are now grown free, and each a tree   15
        With longer growth of our past years;
    But still the grape vine hangs its leaves,
    About the wall between the eaves.

(B) Dear Alice, aye, on twenty years
        Of maiden life, she now has flown;   20
    And oh! that she were here to see
        What then she took to be her own,
    The thing in which we had a right,
    Before we all at last took flight.

(A) As here on this grey bunch of stone   25
        We sat the while the moon, all white,
    Might seem to stop behind the top
        Of yonder cypress, waving light –
    How softly, then, its shade, awhile,
    Would play about her kindly smile!   30

ELIZABETH BARRETT BROWNING

from **Aurora Leigh**

First, the lime

(I had enough, there, of the lime, to be sure, –
My morning dream was often hummed away
By the bees in it); past the lime, the lawn,
Which, after sweeping broadly round the house,   5
Went trickling through the shrubberies in a stream
Of tender turf, and wore and lost itself
Among the acacias, over which you saw
The irregular line of elms by the deep lane
Which stopped the grounds and dammed the overflow   10
Of arbutus and laurel. Out of sight
The lane was; sunk so deep, no foreign tramp
Nor drover of wild ponies out of Wales
Could guess if lady's hall or tenant's lodge
Dispensed such odours . . .   15

ALFRED, LORD TENNYSON

Song

A spirit haunts the year's last hours
Dwelling amid these yellowing bowers:
     To himself he talks;
For at eventide, listening earnestly,
At his work you may hear him sob and sigh   5
     In the walks;
     Earthward he boweth the heavy stalks
Of the mouldering flowers:
     Heavily hangs the broad sunflower
          Over its grave i' the earth so chilly;   10
     Heavily hangs the hollyhock,
          Heavily hangs the tiger-lily.

The air is damp, and hushed, and close,
As a sick man's room when he taketh repose
    An hour before death;   15
My very heart faints and my whole soul grieves
At the moist rich smell of the rotting leaves,
    And the breath
    Of the fading edges of the box beneath,
And the year's last rose.   20
  Heavily hangs the broad sunflower
    Over its grave i' the earth so chilly;
  Heavily hangs the hollyhock,
    Heavily hangs the tiger-lily.

from **In Memoriam A.H.H.**

Unwatched, the garden bough shall sway,
  The tender blossom flutter down,
  Unloved, the beech will gather brown,
This maple burn itself away;

Unloved, the sunflower, shining fair,   5
  Ray round with flames her disk of seed,
  And many a rose-carnation feed
With summer spice the humming air;

Unloved, by many a sandy bar,
  The brook shall babble down the plain,   10
  At noon or when the lesser wain
Is twisting round the polar star;

Uncared for, gird the windy grove,
  And flood the haunts of hern and crake;
  Or into silver arrows break   15
The sailing moon in creek and cove;

Till from the garden and the wild
   A fresh association blow,
   And year by year the landscape grow
Familiar to the stranger's child;   20

As year by year the labourer tills
   His wonted glebe, or lops the glades;
   And year by year our memory fades
From all the circle of the hills.

from **Aylmer's Field**

For out beyond her lodges, where the brook
Vocal, with here and there a silence, ran
By sallowy rim, arose the labourers' homes,
A frequent haunt of Edith, on low knolls
That dimpling died into each other, huts   5
At random scattered, each a nest in bloom.
Her art, her hand, her counsel all had wrought
About them: here was one that, summer-blanched,
Was parcel-bearded with the traveller's-joy
In Autumn, parcel ivy-clad; and here   10
The warm-blue breathings of a hidden hearth
Broke from a bower of vine and honeysuckle:
One looked all rose tree, and another wore
A close-set robe of jasmine sown with stars:
This had a rosy sea of gillyflowers   15
About it; this, a milky-way on earth,
Like visions in the Northern dreamer's heavens,
A lily-avenue climbing to the doors;
One, almost to the martin-haunted eaves
A summer burial deep in hollyhocks;   20
Each, its own charm . . .

ANNE BRONTË

Home

How brightly glittering in the sun
   The woodland ivy plays!
While yonder beech trees from their barks
   Reflect his silver rays.

That sun surveys a lovely scene   5
   From softly smiling skies;
And mildly through unnumbered trees
   The wind of winter sighs:

Now loud, it thunders o'er my head,
   And now in distance dies.   10
But give me back my barren hills
   Where colder breezes rise;

Where scarce the scattered, stunted trees
   Can yield an answering swell,
But where a wilderness of health   15
   Returns the sound as well.

For yonder garden, fair and wide,
   With groves of evergreen,
Long winding walks, and borders trim,
   And velvet lawns between;   20

Restore me to that little spot
   With grey walls compassed round,
Where knotted grass neglected lies,
   And weeds usurp the ground.

Though all around this mansion high   25
   Invites the foot to roam,
And though its halls are fair within –
   Oh, give me back my HOME!

MATTHEW ARNOLD

from **Thyrsis**

So, some tempestuous morn in early June,
　　When the year's primal burst of bloom is o'er,
　　　Before the roses and the longest day –
　　When garden-walks and all the grassy floor
　　　With blossoms red and white of fallen May   5
　　　　And chestnut-flowers are strewn –
So have I heard the cuckoo's parting cry,
　　From the wet field, through the vexed garden-trees,
　　Come with the volleying rain and tossing breeze:
The bloom is gone, and with the bloom go I!   10

Too quick despairer, wherefore wilt thou go?
　　Soon will the high Midsummer pomps come on,
　　　Soon will the musk carnations break and swell,
　　Soon shall we have gold-dusted snapdragon,
　　　Sweet-William with his homely cottage-smell,   15
　　　　And stocks in fragrant blow;
Roses that down the alleys shine afar,
　　And open, jasmine-muffled lattices,
　　And groups under the dreaming garden-trees,
And the full moon, and the white evening-star.   20

He hearkens not! light comer, he is flown!
　　What matters? next year he will return,
　　　And we shall have him in the sweet spring-days,
　　With whitening hedges and uncrumpling fern,
　　　And blue-bells trembling by the forest-ways,   25
　　　　And scent of hay new-mown.
But Thyrsis never more we swains shall see;
　　See him come back, and cut a smoother reed,
　　And blow a strain the world at last shall heed –
For Time, not Corydon, hath conquered thee! . . .   30

GEORGE MEREDITH

from **Love in the Valley**

When at dawn she sighs, and like an infant to the window
  Turns grave eyes craving light, released from dreams,
Beautiful she looks, like a white water-lily
  Bursting out of bud in havens of the streams.
When from bed she rises clothed from neck to ankle   5
  In her long nightgown sweet as boughs of May,
Beautiful she looks, like a tall garden lily
  Pure from the night, and splendid for the day.

Mother of the dews, dark eye-lashed twilight,
  Low-lidded twilight o'er the valley's brim,   10
Rounding on thy breast sings the dew-delighted skylark,
  Clear as though the dew drops had their voice in him.
Hidden where the rose-flush drinks the rayless planet,
  Fountain-full he pours the spraying fountain-showers.
Let me hear her laughter, I would have her ever   15
  Cool as dew in twilight, the lark above the flowers.

All the girls are out with their baskets for the primrose;
  Up lanes, woods through, they troop in joyful bands.
My sweet leads: she knows not why, but now she loiters,
  Eyes the bent anemones, and hangs her hands.   20
Such a look will tell that the violets are peeping,
  Coming the rose: and unaware a cry
Springs in her bosom for odours and for colour,
  Covert and the nightingale; she knows not why.

Kerchiefed head and chin she darts between her tulips,   25
  Streaming like a willow grey in arrowy rain:
Some bend beaten cheek to gravel, and their angel
  She will be; she lifts them, and on she speeds again.
Black the driving raincloud breasts the iron gateway:
  She is forth to cheer a neighbour lacking mirth.   30
So when sky and grass met rolling dumb for thunder
  Saw I once a white dove, sole light of the earth.

Prim little scholars are the flowers of her garden,
   Trained to stand in rows, and asking if they please.
I might love them well but for loving more the wild ones: 35
   O my wild ones! they tell me more than these.
You, my wild one, you tell of honied field-rose,
   Violet, blushing eglantine in life; and even as they,
They by the wayside are earnest of your goodness,
   You are of life's, on the banks that line the way.   40

Peering at her chamber the white crowns the red rose,
   Jasmine winds the porch with stars two and three.
Parted is the window; she sleeps; the starry jasmine
   Breathes a falling breath that carries thoughts of me.
Sweeter unpossessed, have I said of her my sweetest?   45
   Not while she sleeps: while she sleeps the jasmine breathes,
Luring her to love; she sleeps; the starry jasmine
   Bears me to her pillow under white rose-wreaths.

Yellow with birdfoot-trefoil are the grass-glades;
   Yellow with cinquefoil of the dew-grey leaf;   50
Yellow with stone-crop; the moss-mounds are yellow;
   Blue-necked the wheat sways, yellowing to the sheaf.
Green-yellow bursts from the copse the laughing yaffle;
   Sharp as a sickle is the edge of shade and shine;
Earth in her heart laughs looking at the heavens,   55
   Thinking of the harvest: I look and think of mine.

WILLIAM MORRIS

from The Earthly Paradise, August

Across the gap made by our English hinds,
Amidst the Roman's handiwork, behold
Far off the long-roofed church; the shepherd binds
The withy round the hurdles of his fold,
Down in the fosse the river fed of old,   5

That through long lapse of time has grown to be
The little grassy valley that you see.

   Rest here awhile, not yet the eve is still,
The bees are wandering yet, and you may hear
The barley mowers on the trenched hill,   10
The sheep-bells, and the restless changing weir,
All little sounds made musical and clear
Beneath the sky that burning August gives,
While yet the thought of glorious Summer lives.

Ah, love! such happy days, such days as these,   15
Must we still waste them, craving for the best,
Like lovers o'er the painted images
Of those whom once their yearning hearts have blessed?
Have we been happy on our day of rest?
Thine eyes say 'yes,' – but if it came again,   20
Perchance its ending would not seem so vain.

Now came fulfilment of the year's desire,
The tall wheat, coloured by the August fire
Grew heavy-headed, dreading its decay,
And blacker grew the elm-trees day by day.   25
About the edges of the yellow corn,
And o'er the gardens grown somewhat outworn
The bees went hurrying to fill up their store;

The apple-boughs bent over more and more;
With peach and apricot the garden wall   30
Was odorous, and the pears began to fall
From off the high tree with each freshening breeze.
   So in a house bordered about with trees,
A little raised above the waving gold
The Wanderers heard this marvellous story told,   35
While 'twixt the gleaming flasks of ancient wine,
They watched the reapers' slow advancing line.

ALFRED AUSTIN

'Had I a Garden'

Had I a garden, it should lie
    All smiling to the sun,
And after bird and butterfly
    Children should romp and run,
Filling their little laps with flowers,   5
    The air with shout and song,
While golden-crests in guelder bowers
    Rippled the whole day long.

Had I a garden, alleys green
    Should lead where none would guess,   10
Save lovers, to exchange, unseen,
    Shy whisper and caress.
For then the nightingale should sing
    Long after it was June,
And they should kiss and deem it Spring   15
    Under the harvest moon.

Had I a garden, claustral yews
    Should shut out railing wind,
That poets might on sadness muse
    With a majestic mind;   20
With ear attuned and godlike gaze
    Scan Heaven and fathom Hell,
Then through life's labyrinthine maze
    Chant to us, 'All is well!'

Had I a garden, it should grow   25
    Shelter where feeble feet
Might loiter long, or wander slow
    And deem decadence sweet;
Pausing, might ponder on the past,
    Vague twilight in their eyes,   30
Wane calmer, comelier, to the last,
    Then die, as Autumn dies.

ALGERNON CHARLES SWINBURNE

A Forsaken Garden

In a coign of the cliff between lowland and highland,
    At the sea-down's edge between windward and lee,
Walled round with rocks as an inland island,
    The ghost of a garden fronts the sea.
A girdle of brushwood and thorn encloses   5
    The steep square slope of the blossomless bed
Where the weeds that grew green from the graves of its roses
            Now lie dead.

The fields fall southward, abrupt and broken,
    To the low last edge of the long lone land.   10
If a step should sound or a word be spoken,
    Would a ghost not rise at the strange guest's hand?
So long have the grey bare walks lain guestless,
    Through branches and briars if a man make way,
He shall find no life but the sea wind's, restless   15
            Night and day.

The dense hard passage is blind and stifled
    That crawls by a track none turn to climb
To the strait waste place that the years have rifled
    Of all but the thorns that are touched not of time.   20
The thorns he spares when the rose is taken;
    The rocks are left when he wastes the plain.
The wind that wanders, the weeds wind-shaken,
            These remain.

Not a flower to be pressed of the foot that falls not;   25
    As the heart of a dead man the seed-plots are dry;
From the thicket of thorns whence the nightingale calls not,
    Could she call, there were never a rose to reply.
Over the meadows that blossom and wither
    Rings but the note of a sea-bird's song;   30
Only the sun and the rain come hither
            All year long.

The sun burns sere and the rain dishevels
  One gaunt bleak blossom of scentless breath.
Only the wind here hovers and revels   35
  In a round where life seems barren as death.
Here there was laughing of old, there was weeping,
  Haply, of lovers none ever will know,
Whose eyes went seaward a hundred sleeping
          Years ago.   40

Heart handfast in heart as they stood, 'Look thither,'
  Did he whisper? 'Look forth from the flowers to the sea,
For the foam-flowers endure when the rose-blossoms wither,
  And men that love lightly may die – but we?'
And the same wind sang and the same waves whitened,   45
  And or ever the garden's last petals were shed,
In the lips that had whispered, the eyes that had lightened,
          Love was dead.

Or they loved their life through, and then went whither?
  And were one to the end – but what end who knows?   50
Love deep as the sea as a rose must wither,
  As the rose-red seaweed that mocks the rose.
Shall the dead take thought for the dead to love them?
  What love was ever as deep as a grave?
They are loveless now as the grass above them   55
          Or the wave.

All are at one now, roses and lovers,
  Not known of the cliffs and the fields and the sea.
Not a breath of the time that has been hovers
  In the air now soft with a summer to be.   60
Not a breath shall there sweeten the seasons hereafter
  Of the flowers or the lovers that laugh now or weep,
When as they that are free now of weeping and laughter
          We shall sleep.

Here death may deal not again for ever;   65
  Here change may come not till all change end.
From the graves they have made they shall rise up never,
  Who have left nought living to ravage and rend.

Earth, stones, and thorns of the wild ground growing,
   While the sun and the rain live, these shall be;   70
Till a last wind's breath upon all these blowing
        Roll the sea.

Till the slow sea rise and the sheer cliff crumble,
   Till terrace and meadow the deep gulfs drink,
Till the strength of the waves of the high tides humble   75
   The fields that lessen, the rocks that shrink,
Here now in his triumph where all things falter,
   Stretched out on the spoils that his own hand spread,
As a god self-slain on his own strange altar,
        Death lies dead.   80

from **The Mill Garden**

Stately stand the sunflowers, glowing down the garden-side,
Ranged in royal rank arow along the warm grey wall,
Whence their deep disks burn at rich midnoon afire with pride,
Even as though their beams indeed were sunbeams, and the tall
Sceptral stems bore stars whose reign endures, not flowers that
   fall.   5
Lowlier laughs and basks the kindlier flower of homelier fame,
Held by love the sweeter that it blooms in Shakespeare's name,
Fragrant yet as though his hand had touched and made it thrill,
Like the whole world's heart, with warm new life and gladdening
   flame.
Fair befall the fair green close that lies below the mill!   10

HENRY AUSTIN DOBSON

A Garden Song: to W.E.H.

Here, in this sequestered close,
Bloom the hyacinth and rose;
Here, beside the modest stock
Flaunts the flaring hollyhock;
Here, without a pang, one sees   5
Ranks, conditions, and degrees.

All the seasons run their race
In this quiet resting place;
Peach, and apricot, and fig
Here will ripen, and grow big;   10
Here is store and overplus, –
More had not Alcinous!

Here, in alleys cool and green,
Far ahead the thrush is seen;
Here along the southern wall   15
Keeps the bee his festival;
All is quiet else – afar
Sounds of toil and turmoil are.

Here be shadows large and long;
Here be spaces meet for song;   20
Grant, O garden-god, that I,
Now that none profane is nigh, –
Now that mood and moment please, –
Find the fair Pierides!

THOMAS HARDY

During Wind and Rain

They sing their dearest songs –
He, she, all of them – yea,
Treble and tenor and bass,
   And one to play;
With the candles mooning each face. . . .   5
   Ah, no; the years O!
How the sick leaves reel down in throngs!

They clear the creeping moss –
Elders and juniors – aye,
Making the pathways neat   10
   And the garden gay;
And they build a shady seat. . . .
   Ah, no; the years, the years;
See, the white storm-birds wing across.

They are blithely breakfasting all –   15
Men and maidens – yea,
Under the summer tree,
   With a glimpse of the bay,
While pet fowl come to the knee. . . .
   Ah, no; the years O!   20
And the rotten rose is ripped from the wall.

They change to a high new house,
He, she, all of them – aye,
Clocks and carpets and chairs
   On the lawn all day,   25
And brightest things that are thus. . . .
   Ah, no; the years, the years;
Down their carved names the raindrop ploughs.

ROBERT LOUIS STEVENSON

Autumn Fires

In the other gardens
    And all up the vale,
From autumn bonfires
    See the smoke trail!

Pleasant summer over   5
    And all the summer flowers,
The red fire blazes,
    The grey smoke towers.

Sing a song of seasons!
    Something bright in all!   10
Flowers in the summer,
    Fires in the fall!

The Gardener

The gardener does not love to talk,
He makes me keep the gravel walk;
And when he puts his tools away,
He locks the door and takes the key.

Away behind the currant row   5
Where no one else but cook may go,
Far in the plots, I see him dig
Old and serious, brown and big.

He digs the flowers, green, red and blue,
Nor wishes to be spoken to.   10
He digs the flowers and cuts the hay,
And never seems to want to play.

Silly gardener! summer goes,
And winter comes with pinching toes,
When in the garden bare and brown   15
You must lay your barrow down.

Well now, and while the summer stays
To profit by these garden days
O how much wiser you would be
To play at Indian wars with me!   20

OSCAR WILDE

Impressions, I
Le Jardin

The lily's withered chalice falls
    Around its rod of dusty gold,
    And from the beech tree on the wold
The last wood-pigeon coos and calls.

The gaudy leonine sunflower   5
    Hangs black and barren on its stalk,
    And down the wintry garden walk
The dead leaves scatter, – hour by hour.

Pale privet-petals white as milk
    Are blown into a snowy mass;   10
    The roses lie upon the grass,
Like little shreds of crimson silk.

SIR HENRY NEWBOLT

Song

(To An air by Henry Lawes, published in 1652)

The flowers that in thy garden rise,
Fade and are gone when Summer flies,
And as their sweets by time decay,
So shall thy hopes be cast away.

The Sun that gilds the creeping moss   5
Stayeth not Earth's eternal loss:
He is the lord of all that live,
Yet there is life he cannot give.

The stir of Morning's eager breath –
Beautiful Eve's impassioned death –   10
Thou lovest these, thou lovest well,
Yet of the night thou canst not tell.

In every land thy feet may tread,
Time like a veil is round thy head:
Only the land thou seek'st with me   15
Never hath been nor yet shall be.

It is not far, it is not near,
Name it hath none that Earth can hear;
But there thy Soul shall build again
Memories long destroyed of men,   20
And Joy thereby shall like a river
Wander from deep to deep forever.

WALTER DE LA MARE

The Sunken Garden

Speak not – whisper not;
Here bloweth thyme and bergamot:
Softly on the evening hour,
Secret herbs their spices shower
Dark-spiked rosemary and myrrh,   5
Lean-stalked purple lavender;
Hides within her bosom, too,
All her sorrows, bitter rue.

Breathe not – trespass not;
Of this green and darkling spot,   10
Latticed from the moon's beams,
Perchance distant dreamer dreams;
Perchance upon its darkening air
The unseen ghosts of children fare,
Faintly swinging, sway and sweep,   15
Like lovely sea-flowers in the deep;
While, unmoved, to watch and ward,
Amid its gloomed and daisied sward,
Stands with bowed and dewy head
That one little leaden Lad.   20

MARY URSULA BETHELL

Time

'Established' is a good word, much used in garden books,
'The plant, when established' . . .
Oh, become established quickly, quickly, garden!
For I am fugitive, I am very fugitive –

Those that come after me will gather these roses,   5
And watch, as I do now, the white wistaria

Burst, in the sunshine, from its pale green sheath.
Planned. Planted. Established. Then neglected,
Till at last the loiterer by the gate will wonder
At the old, old cottage, the old wooden cottage,   10
And say, 'One might build here, the view is glorious,
This must have been a pretty garden once.'

EDWARD THOMAS

'Old Man, or Lad's-love'

Old Man, or Lad's-love, – in the name there's nothing
To me that knows not Lad's-love, or Old Man,
The hoar-green feathery herb, almost a tree,
Growing with rosemary and lavender.
Even to me that knows it well, the names   5
Half decorate, half perplex, the thing it is:
At least, what that is clings not to the names
In spite of time. And yet I like the names.

The herb itself I like not, but for certain
I love it, as some day the child will love it   10
Who plucks a feather from the door-side bush
Whenever she goes in or out of the house.
Often she waits there, snipping the tips and shrivelling
The shreds at last on to the path, perhaps
Thinking, perhaps of nothing, till she sniffs   15
Her fingers and runs off. The bush is still
But half as tall as she, though it is as old;
So well she clips it. Not a word she says;
And I can only wonder how much hereafter
She will remember, with that bitter scent,   20
Of garden rows, and ancient damson trees
Topping a hedge, a bent path to a door,
A low thick bush beside the door, and me

Forbidding her to pick.
              As for myself,
Where first I met the bitter scent is lost.   25
I, too, often shrivel the grey shreds,
Sniff them and think what it is I am remembering,
Always in vain. I cannot like the scent,
Yet I would rather give up others more sweet,
With no meaning, than this bitter one.   30
I have mislaid the key. I sniff and spray
And think of nothing; I see and hear nothing;
Yet seem, too, to be listening, lying in wait
For what I should, yet never can, remember:
No garden appears, no path, no hoar-green bush   35
Of Lad's-love, or Old Man, no child beside,
Neither father nor mother, nor any playmate;
Only an avenue, dark, nameless, without end.

VITA SACKVILLE-WEST

from **The Land**

When skies are gentle, breezes bland,
When loam that's warm within the hand
Falls friable between the tines,
Sow hollyhocks and columbines,
The tufted pansy, and the tall   5
Snapdragon in the broken wall,
Not for this summer, but for next,
Since foresight is the gardener's text,
And though his eyes may never know
How lavishly his flowers blow,   10
Others will stand and musing say
'These were the flowers he sowed that May.'

But for this summer's quick delight
Sow marigold, and sow the bright

Frail poppy that with noonday dies   15
But wakens to a fresh surprise;
Along the pathway stones be set
Sweet Alysson and mignonette,
That when the full midsummer's come
On scented clumps the bees may hum,   20
Golden Italians, and the wild
Black bumble-bee alike beguiled:
And lovers who have never kissed
May sow the cloudy Love-in-Mist.

Nor be the little space forgot   25
For herbs to spice the kitchen pot:
Mint pennyroyal, bergamot,
Tarragon and melilot,
Dill for witchcraft, prisoner's rue,
Coriander, costmary,   30
Tansy, thyme, Sweet Cicely,
Saffron, balm, and rosemary
That since the Virgin threw her cloak
Across it, – so say cottage folk –
Has changed its flowers from white to blue.   35
But have a care that seeds be strewn
One night beneath a waxing moon,
And pick when the moon is on the wane,
Else shall your toil be all in vain . . .

from The Garden, Autumn

Autumn in felted slipper shuffles on,
Muted yet fiery, – Autumn's character.
Brown as a monk yet flaring as a whore,
And in the distance blue as Raphael's robe
Tender around the Virgin.
                              Blue the smoke   5
Drifting across brown woods; but in the garden

Maples are garish, and surprising leaves
Make sudden fires with sudden crests of flame
Where the sun hits them; in the deep-cut leaf
Of peony, like a mediaeval axe   10
Of rusty iron; fervour of azalea
Whose dying days repeat her June of flower;
In Sargent's cherry, upright as a torch
Till ravelled sideways by the wind to stream
Disorderly, and strew the mint of sparks   15
In coins of pointed metal, cooling down;
And that true child of Fall, whose morbid fruit
Ripens, with walnuts, only in November,
The Medlar lying brown across the thatch;
Rough elbows of rough branches, russet fruit   20
So blet it's worth no more than sleepy pear,
But in its motley pink and yellow leaf
A harlequin that some may overlook
Nor ever think to break and set within
A vase of bronze against a wall of oak,   25
With Red-hot Poker, Autumn's final torch . . .

ELIZABETH JENNINGS

Night Garden of the Asylum

An owl's call scrapes the stillness.
Curtains are barriers and behind them
The beds settle into neat rows.
Soon they'll be ruffled.

The garden knows nothing of illness.   5
Only it knows of the slow gleam
Of stars, the moon's distilling; it knows
Why the beds and lawns are levelled.

Then all is broken from its fullness.
A human cry cuts across a dream.   10
A wild hand squeezes an open rose.
We are in witchcraft, bedevilled.

ANNE STEVENSON

The Garden

She feels it like a shoulder of hair,
the garden, shrugging off the steamed, squeezed
eye of her kitchen window. Self-engendered chaos,
milky convulvulus, huge comet daisies. Tear
open the stocking of the leek pod and it frees   5
mathematically its globe, its light radiants.

But still she feels it hateful, August in its sweat,
the children filthy and barefoot . . . angry woman
in a stained striped apron, sipping juice off a knife,
thick syrups of pounded rose hip and pulped fruit.   10
In bright air, between briar roses and a viney drain,
Arenea diadema sips the silk-spinkled fly.

Her pet cat's a killer, a fur muff
curled fatly now in a catnest of hot
grass and goutweed. Of this morning's robin   15
too much was left – feathers, fluff,
feet, beak, the gorgeous throat caught
in the gored, delicate, perfectly balanced skeleton.

Notes

Note: editorial titles in square brackets.
Geoffrey Chaucer *c.*1340–1400

[*The Garden of Mirth*]: from his translation of Guillaume de Lorris's mid-thirteenth-century *Roman de la Rose* (*Romance of the Rose*), Fragment A, ll.1349–86, 1409–12, 1424–38. **2 compassing:** shape. **4 charge:** load. **5 But . . . tree:** except for trees too ugly [for the garden]. **7 wot:** know. **11 foison:** plenty. **14 withal:** also. **15 alemanders:** almonds. **17 waxen:** grew. **19 eke:** also. **20 clove-gillyflower:** clove (from Old French *clou de girofle*, girofle nail). **21 Grain de Parays:** grains of paradise (the capsules of the West African meleguetta tree, *Amomum meleguetta*). **22 Canel . . . price:** cinnamon and valuable zedoary. **28 fain:** fond. **29 aleys:** serviceberries; **bullace:** semi-wild plums. **32 ranged clean:** filled with abundant rows. **45 mister was:** was needful. **47 such a grace:** so well favoured. **54 quaint:** artfully planted.

Mum and the Soothsayer. Early fifteenth century, BL MS Add 41666; first printed for the Early English Text Society, 1936 (ed. M. Day and R. Steele). A poem on the condition of England under Henry IV: the principle of 'keeping mum' (quiet on matters of importance) is ruining society; truth-telling (soothsaying) must prevail against it. In the excerpt here (ll. 946–56, 976–91), the narrator's dream of a well-ordered garden contrasts with the state of England (as in Shakespeare's *Richard II*, III. iv; and cf. **Marvell, Appleton House**, pp. 39–42). **3 franklin:** freeman landowner. **4 bode:** waited. **5 gome:** man. **7 imps:** saplings; **herbs:** plants; **fele:** many. **12 soothly:** in truth; **sith:** since; **bore:** born. **14 garth:** garden. **16 longeth:** belong; **leighton:** garden; **the law . . . do:** I will do [only] what is lawful. **18 worms:** creeping creatures (snails, slugs, etc.). **23 travailen:** work; **twint:** jot, iota. **26 trow:** believe. **29 prettiest:** most skilful. (The beehive as an emblem of the well-ordered state goes back at least as far as Virgil, *Georgics*, IV).

William Dunbar c.1460–c.1520

'*Sweet Rose of Virtue*' exists in several manuscript and later printed sources. **1 gentless:** nobility. **2 lustiness:** delight; gay attire. **6 garth:** garden; **pursue:** proceed. **10 rue:** the herb; also, regret. **12 mene:** complain. **14 make:** also, compose (a poem).

John Skelton c.1460–1529

To Mistress Isabel Pennell: from *Garland or Chaplet of Laurel* (1523). **5 Reflairing:** scent-emitting; **rosabel:** beautiful rose (nonce use). **7 rosary:** rose-plot. **10 nept:** catmint. **11 gillyflower:** clove-scented pink (cf. Chaucer, line 20n.). **12 proper:** comely. **13 Ennewed:** tinted. **17 spray:** bough.

Anon c.1500

'*This day day daws*': carol, in various manuscripts. Perhaps in honour of Henry VII's queen, Margaret of York (the white rose). **1 daws:** dawns. **8 between:** among [them]. **14 gent:** noble. **15 flower-de-luce:** fleur-de-lis (iris), emblem of France; **on rue:** have pity on.

Thomas Howell fl.1560s

The Rose: from *The Arbour of Amity* (1568).

George Gascoigne c.1540–77

Inscription in a Garden: from *A Hundred Sundry Flowers* (1573).

Edmund Spenser ?1552–99

[*The Garden of Adonis*]: from *The Fairy Queen* (1590), Book III, canto vi. The title anciently signified a place of fruitful, fast-growing plants. Adonis, a vegetation god and Venus's beloved, was killed by a boar. **1 She:** Venus. **2 wones:** inhabits. **5 wote:** know. **13 seminary:** seed plot. **17 weeds:** plants. **22 That:** so that. **24 moten:** might. **26 Genius:** god of generation. **32 weeds:** clothing. **33 list:** pleases. **42 hue:** shape. **43 Or:** before [being]. **50–1 Which . . . multiply:** Genesis 1:22, 28. **54 imply:** are full up with. **56 uncouth:** strange. **59 reasonable:** rational; **endue:** put on. **76 invade:** enter. **86 temper:** disposition; **complexion:** constitution. **88 kind:** nature. **93 addressed:** equipped. **106 n'ote:** knew not how to;

despite: malice. **114 fell:** cruel; **fond:** foolish. **115 Frankly:** freely; **leman:** beloved. **121 wanton:** frolicsome; **prime:** spring. **122 eke:** also; **at once:** at the same time.

Sonnet: Amoretti (1595), no. 64. Compare the opening kiss and flower imagery of Song of Solomon, 1, 2. **4 bowers:** bedchambers. **7 bellamours:** Spenserian nonce word meaning 'beautiful loves'. **12 jessamines:** jasmine (which, like all the flowers in the poem, symbolises love).

George Chapman *c*.1559–1634

Ovid's Banquet of Sense (1595), ll. 60–90. **12 young . . . desire:** Paris, the Trojan prince who awarded her the prize for beauty. **15 Chloris:** the Roman flower goddess, Flora, in her pre-bloom green state. **16 melanthy:** gith, or *Nigella sativa* (reputedly good against bee stings). **17 Amareus:** perhaps Amaracus, a kind of marjoram. **19 Dian's arrow:** Artemisia (includes common wormwood and southernwood); **Cupid's . . . shield:** love-in-idleness (violet). **20 Ope-morn:** bindweed; **Venus' navel:** pennywort. **22 calamint:** catmint. **23 nepenthe:** the ancient (Egyptian) drug of forgetfulness. **24 rumex:** dock. **25 Sya:** syve (chive); **Furies:** snake-headed underworld goddesses of vengeance. **26 merry:** black cherry; **melliphill:** balm (?). **27 crown imperiaL:** the noble *Fritillaria imperialis* (see Penelope Hobhouse, *Plants in Garden History* (London: Pavilion, 1992), pp. 96–7). **28 amaranth:** anciently an imaginary everlasting flower; by mid-sixteenth century identified with love-lies-bleeding; **asphodel:** white daffodil. **29 twillpants:** unidentified; but I think snake's-head fritillary (*F. meleagris*) because of its chequered pattern (*twill*), and its cup-like flower and wild habitat (appropriate to woodland Bacchus, god of wine).

Michael Drayton 1563–1631

Endymion and Phoebe (1595), ll. 23–66. **2 clip:** embrace. **12 Alcides:** Hercules. **20 Hesperides:** the fabled western gardens where golden apples were guarded by a dragon. **28 orient:** bright; eastern (the best pearls reputedly came from India). **29 eglantine:** hedge rose. **34 ouzel:** blackbird; **mavis:** song-thrush. **37 Zephyr:** west wind of spring who made Chloris (**Chapman, 15n.**) pregnant with flowers. **40 amaranthus: Chapman, 28n.; gillyflowers: Skelton, 11n.**

William Shakespeare 1564–1616

[*Boy's Song*]: from *Two Noble Kinsmen* (?1612), I.i. **7 Ver:** spring.
12 Larks'-heels: larkspur. **20 chough:** jackdaw.

Thomas Campion ?1567–1619

'*There is a Garden in Her Face*': from *The Third and Fourth Book of Airs*
(?1617) **8 orient:** Drayton 28n.

Sir John Davies 1569–1626

Hymns of Astraea (1599), *Hymn* 7. Each hymn is an acrostic on Elisabetha
Regina, Elizabeth I, the Tudor rose.

Aemilia Lanyer 1569–1645

Description of Cookham, ll. 1–80, 127–146, 195–210: from *Salve deus rex
Judaeorum* [Hail Lord, King of the Jews] (1611). The poem's dedicatee is
Margaret Clifford, Countess of Cumberland (d. 1616), whose brother had
stayed at Cookham, a royal manor near Maidenhead, Berkshire, in 1603.
2 Grace: the Countess of Cumberland. **5 indite:** write. **6 story:** i.e., the
volume *Salve rex* . . . . **17 against . . . came:** in anticipation of your coming
thither. **31 Philomela:** the nightingale. **44 phoenix:** marvel (**Robert
Heath, On Clarastella, 26n.** below). **64 defended:** kept off [the sun].
85 inkling: intimation. **86 frame:** form. **95 vain:** pointless. **99 rivelled:**
wrinkled; **rind:** frost; bark.

Ben Jonson c. 1572–1637

To Penshurst: from *The Forest* (1612). **Title: Penshurst,** near Tonbridge,
Kent, was the home of Sir Robert Sidney, Viscount Lisle. **2 touch:** black
marble. **4 lantern:** kind of glazed cupola. **7 marks:** features. **10 dryads:**
tree deities. **11 Pan:** Milton, *Paradise Lost*, 60–1n. below; **Bacchus:**
Chapman, *Ovid's Banquet* . . . , 29n. above. **13 tree:** oak reputedly grown
from an acorn planted at Sir Philip Sidney's birth in 1554. **15 writhed:**
twisted. **16 sylvan:** country lover; **flames:** of love (the ref. is to Sidney's love
sonnets, *Astrophil and Stella* (1591)). **17 satyrs:** lustful goat-men, inhabi-
tants of the woods and companions of **Bacchus;** virtually identical to **fauns**.
19 Gamage: Barbara Gamage had married Robert Sidney in 1584.
25 conies: rabbits. **30 mess:** dining table. **31 Medway:** river in Kent.

34 kind: species. **36 officiously:** dutifully. **40 hours:** Milton, *Paradise Lost*, **60–1n.** below. **48 clown:** rustic. **49 empty-handed:** i.e., not bearing a gift. **56 plum:** fidelity; **pear:** love (because heart-shaped). **67 tells:** counts. **70 Below:** below-stairs (servants' quarters). **73 livery:** provisions. **76 King James:** king of England after death of Elizabeth I in 1603. **77 brave:** handsome; **son:** Prince Henry (died November 1612). **78 as:** as if. **79 penates:** household gods. **82 sudden:** prompt. **87 dressed:** prepared. **98 mysteries:** skills. **99 proportion:** compare.

William Browne of Tavistock *c.*1590–*c.*1645

Vision, V: from *Britannia's Pastorals* (1613–; Book 3 remained unfinished at his death).

Robert Herrick 1591–1674

A Meditation and *To . . . Lady Abdie:* from *Hesperides* (1648).
Meditation **4** July–flower: gillyflower (**Skelton 11n.**); and see *To . . . Lady Abdie,* 3.

To . . . Lady Abdie: **6** jessamine: Spenser, **Sonnet 12n. 23** warden: baking pear known from *c.* 1400.

Christ's Sadness: from *Noble Numbers* (1647). On the garden of Gethsemane (Matthew 26, Mark 14).

George Herbert 1593–1633

Paradise and *Peace:* from *The Temple* (1633).
Paradise: original spelling kept for terminal words.

Peace **15** crown imperial: **Chapman 27n.;** emblem of secular authority. **22–3** prince . . . Salem: Melchizedek, type of Christ (Genesis 14, Hebrews 7). **28** twelve stalks: the disciples. **37–9** Take . . . bread: the Last Supper (e.g., Matthew 26:26) and the Eucharist.

Thomas Carew ?1593–1640

The Enquiry: from *Poems* (1640). **1** myrtles: dedicated to Venus.

James Shirley 1596–1666

The Garden: from *Poems* (1646).

Sir Thomas Browne 1605–82

'The almond flourisheth': first published 1919; from *Works*, ed. G. Keynes, 3 (1964). **2 blow**: bloom. **3 flowery ... seen**: crocus flowering before leaves appear. **8 paronychions**: whitlow-wort.

John Milton 1608–74

[*Eden*]: *Paradise Lost*, IV. 207–68. See Genesis 3. **5 Auran**: Haran (Ezekiel 27:23). **6 Seleucia**: built by Alexander the Great's general, Seleucis Nicator. **8 Telassar**: Isaiah 37:11–12. **13 blooming**: making flourish; **ambrosial**: scented; immortal. **14 vegetable**: living. **22 kindly thirst**: natural desire. **31 crisped**: ruffled. **32 orient**: Drayton 28n. **33 error**: irregular course. **35 nice**: too-fastidious. **36 boon**: bountiful. **44 Hesperian**: Drayton 20n. **49 irriguous**: well-watered; **store**: abundance. **50 without ... rose**: Genesis 3:18. **58 apply**: attend to. **60–1 Pan ... Hours**: Pan was the Graeco-Roman nature god; the three **Graces**, daughters of Zeus, attended Venus, goddess of love and fertility; the **Hours** symbolised the seasons; **knit**: clasping hands.

Joseph Beaumont 1616–99

The Garden: written 1652; first published in *Poems*, ed. E. Robinson (1914). For the details, see Genesis 3. **9 cross**: frustrating. **34 barricadoed**: barred. **36 Calvary**: Luke 23:33.

Rowland Watkyns *c.*1616–64

The Gardener: from *Flamma sinne fumo* (1662). **1 prevents**: precedes.

Abraham Cowley 1618–67

The Wish: from *The Mistress* (1647).

Robert Heath fl. 1650

On Clarastella ...: from *Clarastella; Together with Poems Occasional* (1650). **1 Flora**: Chapman 15n. **5 Ceres**: Roman goddess of harvest; **store**: plenty. **12 reflexed**: reflected. **26 phoenix**: fabled Arabian bird said to die in a nest

of spices out of which its successor was born. **29 turnsole:** heliotrope.
38 sweets: perfumes.

Andrew Marvell 1621–78

Upon Appleton House: To My Lord Fairfax, stanzas 36–45, 84–88: from
Miscellaneous Poems (1681). In the early 1650s Marvell was employed to
teach languages to the daughters of Fairfax, who had retired to his
Yorkshire estate of Nun Appleton after his resignation as commander-in-
chief of the Parliamentary forces in June 1650. **1 the hero:** the son of the
marriage, just mentioned in the poem, between William Fairfax and
Isabella Thwaites in 1518; but the poem's dedicatee, Lord General Thomas
Fairfax, also fought in France. **12 dian:** reveille (French). **15 pan:** part of
the musket lock. **21 virgin nymph:** Mary, born 1638, daughter of Fairfax
and his wife Anne, and the subject of ll. 81–120. **23 compare:** vie.
46 flaming sword: paradise after man's expulsion (Genesis 3:24).
48 waste: the reference is to the Civil War (the subject, indeed, of the whole
poem). **53 arms:** thorns (as a result of the Fall: Genesis 3:18). **55–6 Tulips
... guard:** referring to the red, yellow and black stripes of the Swiss papal
guard. **61 stoves:** i.e., hot houses. **69 Cinque Ports:** the five south-eastern
coastal towns, originally Hastings, Sandwich, Dover, Romney, and Hythe,
under the charge of a Lord Warden, were, during the interregnum, the
responsibility of the Council of State, of which Fairfax was a member. (The
phrase was also used of the five senses: see l. 8). **71 spanned:** restrained.
76 want: lack; need. **78 As ... touch:** the sensitive plant (*Mimosa
pudica*). **84 eben shuts:** ebony shutters. **85 halcyon:** kingfisher; blue, and
therefore an emblem of (the Virgin) Mary. **87 horror:** thrill of awe; rippling
of water. **91 compacts:** solidifies. **92 If:** as if. **100 star new-slain:** meteor
(on occasions thought to be **exhaled** fron the earth). **104 vitrified:** turned to
glass (purified). **118 look:** observe (the *glass* is an attribute of Venus, one of
the goddesses of gardens).

The Garden and *The Mower ...*: from *Miscellaneous Poems* (1681).
The Garden **1 amaze:** perplex. **2 palm ... bays:** for military, civic and
poetic achievement respectively. **5 verged:** extended. **6 upbraid:** reprove;
bind with twigs (for garlands). **7 close:** join. **15–16 rude/To:** uncivil
compared to. **17 white ... red:** traditional colours for beloved's complex-
ion. **18 amorous:** lovely. **19 Fond:** besotted. **25 run ... heat:** exhausted its
ardour. **29 Apollo ... Daphne:** the god of the sun and poetry pursued
Daphne; she was saved by being turned into a laurel. **31 Pan ... Syrinx:**

Pan (Milton 60–1n.) lusted after **Syrinx**, who became a reed (the pan pipe, emblem of pastoral verse). **17 curious:** delicate. **47–8 Annihilating . . . To:** reducing the created world to nothing compared to. **49 sliding:** sloping. **51 vest:** covering (the **bird** symbolises the soul). **54 whets:** preens. **57–8 Such . . . mate:** Eden (until, at Genesis 2:18, God creates 'an *help meet* [suitable] for' Adam). **66 dial:** sundial.

The Mower against Gardens **1 Luxurious:** voluptuous; **in use:** into a habit. **15–16 Its . . . sold:** at the height of contemporary tulip mania a bulb sold in Holland for 5,500 florins. **18 'Marvel of Peru':** *Mirabilis jalapa.* **21–2 Had . . . see:** grafting; and Deuteronomy 22:9.

Henry Vaughan 1622–95

Regeneration: from *Silex Scintillans* (1650). **1 A . . . bonds:** still bound a prisoner to sin. **9 Stormed:** the victim of [internal and external] storms. **23 smoke:** vanities (heavier than the toil up the hill). **27 east:** symbolising spiritual rebirth. **28 Jacob's bed:** Genesis 28:11ff (dream of ladder with angels ascending and descending). **45 spice:** see epigraph from Song of Solomon 4. **49 fountain:** John 4:14. **55 stones:** souls? **60 centre:** the Earth; or hell at the centre of the Earth. **70 wind:** John 3:8; Acts 2:1–2.

Margaret Cavendish, Duchess of Newcastle 1623–73

A Landscape: from *Poems, and Fancies* (1653). **4 champians:** open country. **14 close:** secret. **18–19 hay . . . death:** Isaiah 40 (flesh is grass); Death the reaper. **22 gravel:** small stones; deposits of urinary crystals. **23 gouts:** streams; the disease. **38 Narcissus:** the flower; the Roman mythological self-lover transformed into the flower. **42 bullace: Chaucer 29n. 45 pearplum:** kinds of plum.

N. Hookes (Christian name unknown) 1628–1712

To Amanda Walking in the Garden: from *Amanda* (1653). **8 blows:** blooms. **14 Flora: Chapman 15n. 18 Into . . . spring:** they grow into a stage set presenting a royal progress. **26 fig . . . apron:** Genesis 3:7.

Charles Cotton 1630–87

[Chatsworth]: from *The Wonders of the Peak* (1681). ll.1417–47. The

sixteenth-century house and grounds were substantially remodelled in the
later seventeenth century. **3 plat:** patch of ground. **5 rose:** the Tudor rose
(**Sir John Davies note**). **13 wassail days:** the lament for a lost 'merry
England' is particularly strong in Civil War and Restoration poetry.
21 Icarian: Icarus, ignoring paternal warnings, flew too close to the sun
with his waxen wings; they melted and he drowned (Graeco-Roman myth).
29 naumachies: sea-battles (common feature of pageant and triumphal
entry).

Alexander Pope 1688–1744

The Gardens of Alcinous: translation of Homer, *Odyssey*, VII; in *Guardian*,
no. 173 (1713); then included in Pope's *Odyssey* (1725), VII. 142–75. A
celebrated classical counterpart of Eden. **15 blow:** flower. **24 discoloured:**
pale.
Epistle to Burlington (1731), ll. 47–72, 99–126. **17 intending:** leading
the eye on. **24 Stowe:** Viscount Cobham's show garden, designed by
Charles Bridgeman and William Kent with temples by James Gibbs, Sir John
Vanbrugh and Kent; later modified by 'Capability' Brown (see **Cowper
23n.**). **71 Versailles:** Pope had praised André Le Nôtre (who redesigned the
grounds in the later seventeenth century) in the line before this excerpt
begins. **26 Nero:** presumably his Golden House. **27 Timon:** aristocratic
false taste. **104 Brobdingnag:** land of giants (Swift, *Gulliver's Travels*
(1726), Book II). **51 Amphitrite:** wife of Roman sea-god Neptune.

James Thomson 1700–48

Spring, ll. 904–25; ll. 950-62: from *The Seasons* (1746). **3 Lyttleton:**
George Lyttleton (died 1773), friend and patron of Thomson, Pope and
others. Thomson revised *The Seasons* at **Hagley**, Lyttleton's estate in
Worcestershire. **5 Tempe:** paradisal valley in Thessaly.

William Shenstone 1714–63

The Schoolmistress (1742), st 11–13. **8 gill:** Skelton 11n. **10 euphrasy:**
Euphrasia officinalis, Eyebright. **24 wassail days:** Cotton 13n.

William Mason 1724–97

The English Garden (1771–81), Book III, ll. 108–31; 137–47; 188–205;
252–87 (text from W. Mason, *The English Garden: A Poem in Four Books*,

New edn, corrected, to which are added a commentary and notes by W. Burgh (York, 1783)). **3 this . . . end:** shade and wall cover. **15–16 East . . . plant:** 'our common laurel was first brought into the Low Countries AD1576 (together with horse chestnut) from Constantinople as a present from David Ungnad, the Imperial Ambassador in Turkey, to Clusius the famous Botanist . . .' (Burgh's note); the Roman (**Latian**) bay, symbolising imperial power and victory, was worn by **Julius** Caesar, etc. **36 Dryad:** tree spirit. **42 Maia:** May (i.e., May Day festivities). **48 Disparted:** separated. **55 Augusta:** traditional pageant name for London (emphasises the worth of 'Old England' against foreign imports: compare **Albion** (ancient name for England) at l. 75). **74 Gilead's balm:** Jeremiah 8:22, 46:11. **83 Boreas:** the north wind. **87 penthouse:** shelter with sloping roof; here, greenhouse.

William Cowper 1731–1800

The Task, Book III, ll. 566–87, 765–80. **11 amomum:** cardamom, or the meleguetta tree (**Chaucer 21n.**). **14 Ficoides:** ice-plant (*Mesembrianthemum crystallinum*). **17 Ausonia:** Lower Italy. **19 jessamine: Spenser, Sonnet 12n. 20 Caffraia:** Kafiristan. **22 Orphean:** Orpheus, the Graeco-Roman mythological poet and musician, could move nature with his playing. **23 Brown:** Lancelot 'Capability' Brown (1715–83), the not-always-celebrated landscape 'improver'.

Susan Blamire 1747–94

'When Home We Return': c. 1790; from *The Poetical Works* (Edinburgh, 1842).

William Blake 1757–1827

To Autumn: from *Poetical Sketches* (1783).

Milton, Book the Second (1804–10), plate 31, ll. 28–63. **18 Beulah:** Innocence; Mother Nature; **Ololon:** the poet Milton's creative achievement. **22 Og, Anak:** Numbers 21:33–5 and 13:33.

William Wordsworth 1770–1850

A Flower Garden (1824); published in *Poems* (1827). **7 moving creatures:** Genesis 1:20–1. **12 half-blown:** half-open bud.

"This Lawn . . ." (1829); published in *Yarrow Revisited and Other Poems* (1835).

Samuel Taylor Coleridge 1772–1834

Reflections on Having Left a Place of Retirement: from the *Monthly Magazine*, October 1796. The cottage was at Clevedon. **12 Bristowa's:** Bristol's. **19 viewless:** invisible. **45 While . . . bled:** France declared war on England and Holland in February 1793. **49 Howard:** the prison reformer John Howard (?1726–90), author of *State of the Prisons* (1777). **56 The . . . tribe:** poets.

Thomas Moore 1779–1852

"Tis the Last Rose of Summer': from *Irish Melodies* (1813).

John Keats 1795–1821

'I Stood Tip-toe . . .' (1816), ll. 29–60; published in *Poems* (1817). **21 Apollo:** Graeco-Roman god of the sun and poetry.

The Fall of Hyperion. A Dream, Canto 1, ll. 19–34. Written 1819; first published in Lord Houghton, *Biographical and Historical Miscellanies of the Philobiblon Society*, 1856.

William Barnes 1801–86

The Old Garden (1868): from *Poems* (1908).

Elizabeth Barrett Browning 1806–61

From *Aurora Leigh: A Poem* (1856).

Alfred, Lord Tennyson 1809–92

Song: written at Somersby, Lincolnshire; published in *Poems, Chiefly Lyrical* (1830).

In Memoriam A[rthur] H[enry] H[allam], poem 101 (1850). **22 glebe:** soil.
Aylmer's Field, ll. 145–65; published in *Enoch Arden* (1864).

Anne Brontë 1820–49

Home: published in *Poems by Currer, Ellis and Acton Bell* (1846).

Matthew Arnold 1822–88

Thyrsis (1866), ll. 51–80; published in *New Poems* (1867); in memory of the poet Clough (d. 1861). **30 Corydon:** Virgil, *Eclogues*, 7 (Corydon beats Thyrsis in a singing contest).

George Meredith 1828–1909

Love in the Valley (1878) ll. 65–120: from *Poems and Lyrics of the Joy of Earth* (1883).

William Morris 1834–96

August from *The Earthly Paradise* (1868–70).

Alfred Austin 1835–1913

'Had I a Garden . . .': from *The Garden That I Love* (1894).

Algernon Charles Swinburne 1837–1909

A Forsaken Garden: from *Poems and Ballads, Second Series* (1878).
The Mill Garden, ll. 1–10: from *A Midsummer Holiday* (1884). **7 blooms . . . name:** sweet william.

Henry Austin Dobson 1840–1921

A Garden Song: from *At the Sign of the Lyre* (1885). Dedicated to the critic, poet and dramatist W.E. Henley (1849–1903). **12 Alcinous:** see **Pope, The Gardens of Alcinous,** above. **22 none . . . nigh:** Virgil, *Aeneid*, VI. 258 ('Hence, profane ones'). **24 Pierides:** the Muses (from Mount Pierus in Thrace).

Thomas Hardy 1840–1928

During Wind and Rain: from *Moments of Vision* (1917).

Robert Louis Stevenson 1850–94

Autumn Fires; The Gardener: from *A Child's Garden of Verses* (1885).

Oscar Wilde 1854–1900

Impressions, I: Le Jardin; published in *Our Continent*, vol. I (15 February 1882).

Sir Henry John Newbolt 1862–1938

Song: from *Poems: Old and New* (1912; rev. edn 1919).

Walter de la Mare 1873–1956

The Sunken Garden: from *Motley and Other Poems* (1918).

Mary Ursula Bethell 1874–1945

Time: from *Collected Poems*, as reprinted in *The Faber Book of 20th Century Women's Poetry*, ed. Fleur Adcock (1987).

Edward Thomas 1878–1917

'Old Man, or Lad's-Love': from *Collected Poems* (1936).

Vita Sackville-West 1892–1962

From *Spring*: from *The Land* (1927)
From *Autumn*: from *The Garden* (1946)

Elizabeth Jennings 1926–

Night Garden of the Asylum (1966): from *Collected Poems 1953–1985* (1986).

Anne Stevenson 1933–

The Garden: from *Minute by Glass Minute* (1974).

Acknowledgements

The editor and publishers wish to thank the following for permission to use copyright material:

Curtis Brown, London, on behalf of the Estate of the author for excerpts from Vita Sackville-West, 'The Land' and 'The Garden'; David Higham Associates on behalf of the author for Elizabeth Jennings, 'Night Garden of the Asylum' from *Collected Poems*, Carcanet; Peter Newbolt for an excerpt from Henry Newbolt, 'Song (To an air by Henry Lawes, 1652)' from the Masque, 'Dream-Market' (written for performance at Wilton House, near Salisbury, and performed on 28th July 1909) included in *Poems: New and Old*, John Murray, 1912; Oxford University Press for Anne Stevenson, 'The Garden' from *The Collected Poems of Anne Stevenson 1955–1995*, 1996; The Society of Authors as the representative of the Literary Trustees of the author for Walter de la Mare, 'The Sunken Garden' from *The Complete Poems of Walter de la Mare*, 1969.

Every effort has been made to trace the copyright holders but if any have been inadvertently overlooked the publishers will be pleased to make the necessary arrangement at the first opportunity.

Everyman's Poetry

Titles available in this series

William Blake
ed. Peter Butter
0 460 87800 X

The Brontës
ed. Pamela Norris
0 460 87864 6

**Rupert Brooke &
Wilfred Owen**
ed. George Walter
0 460 87801 8

**Elizabeth Barrett
Browning**
ed. Colin Graham
0 460 87894 8

Robert Browning
ed. Colin Graham
0 460 87893 X

Robert Burns
ed. Donald Low
0 460 87814 X

Lord Byron
ed. Jane Stabler
0 460 87810 7

Geoffrey Chaucer:
Comic and Bawdy Tales
ed. Malcolm Andrew
0 460 87869 7

John Clare
ed. R. K. R. Thornton
0 460 87823 9

Arthur Hugh Clough
ed. John Beer
0 460 87939 1

Samuel Taylor Coleridge
ed. John Beer
0 460 87826 3

Dante
ed. Anna Lawrence
0 460 87955 3

Emily Dickinson
ed. Helen McNeil
0 460 87895 6

John Donne
ed. D. J. Enright
0 460 87901 4

John Dryden
ed. David Hopkins
0 460 87940 5

Four Metaphysical Poets
ed. Douglas Brooks-Davies
0 460 87857 3

Oliver Goldsmith
ed Robert L. Mack
0 460 87827 1

Thomas Gray
ed. Robert L. Mack
0 460 87805 0

Ivor Gurney
ed. George Walter
0 460 87797 6

Thomas Hardy
ed. Norman Page
0 460 87956 1

Heinrich Heine
ed. T. J. Reed
& David Cram
0 460 87865 4

George Herbert
ed. D. J. Enright
0 460 87795 X

Robert Herrick
ed. Douglas Brooks-Davies
0 460 87799 2

John Keats
ed. Nicholas Roe
0 460 87808 5

Omar Khayyám
ed. Tony Briggs
0 460 87954 5

Rudyard Kipling
ed. Jan Hewitt
0 460 87941 3

**Henry Wadsworth
Longfellow**
ed. Anthony Thwaite
0 460 87821 2

Andrew Marvell
ed. Gordon Campbell
0 460 87812 3

John Milton
ed. Gordon Campbell
0 460 87813 1

More Poetry Please!
Foreword by P. J.
Kavanagh
0 460 87899 9

Edgar Allan Poe
ed. Richard Gray
0 460 87804 2

Poetry Please!
Foreword by
Charles Causley
0 460 87824 7

Alexander Pope
ed. Douglas Brooks-
Davies
0 460 87798 4

Alexander Pushkin
ed. A. D. P. Briggs
0 460 87862 X

Lord Rochester
ed. Paddy Lyons
0 460 87819 0

Christina Rossetti
ed. Jan Marsh
0 460 87820 4

William Shakespeare
ed. Martin Dodsworth
0 460 87815 8

Percy Bysshe Shelley
ed. Timothy Webb
0 460 87944 8

John Skelton
ed. Greg Walker
0 460 87796 8

R. L. Stevenson
ed. Jenni Calder
0 460 87809 3

Jonathan Swift
ed. Michael Bruce
0 460 87945 6

**Algernon Charles
Swinburne**
ed. Catherine Maxwell
0 460 87871 9

Alfred, Lord Tennyson
ed. Michael Baron
0 460 87802 6

Dylan Thomas
ed. Walford Davies
0 460 87831 X

Edward Thomas
ed. William Cooke
0 460 87877 8

R. S. Thomas
ed. Anthony Thwaite
0 460 87811 5

Walt Whitman
ed. Ellman Crasnow
0 460 87825 5

Oscar Wilde
ed. Robert Mighall
0 460 87803 4

William Wordsworth
ed. Stephen Logan
0 460 87946 4

W. B. Yeats
ed. John Kelly
0 460 87902 2